David

Happy Birthday

1989

FAX 2 DA MAX

Written by **J**erry **H**opkins

Designed by **S**unny **P**auole

Cover by **D**enise **R**atliff

Published by
THE BESS PRESS, INC.
P.O. BOX 22388
HONOLULU, HI 96822

INTRODUCTION

This is the second volume of Hawaiian lists and trivia. The first, *Fax to Da Max: Everything You Didn't Know You Wanted to Know About Hawaii*, was the bestselling local book of 1985. It was created by Jerry Hopkins with Doug "Peppo" Simonson, Pat Sasaki and Ken Sakata.

Peppo is now one artiste! (With shows in California taking up his time.) Pat is a working mother. (A novel in the works and two children to raise.) And Ken has disappeared. (Na na na, he's on the Mainland getting rich.) That left Jerry, who did this book pretty much alone.

Jerry also writes speeches for Mayor Frank Fasi and frequently sees one of his rock and roll biographies (Elvis Presley, Jim Morrison, David Bowie, Jimi Hendrix) on the international bestseller lists. With his wife, Rebecca Crockett-Hopkins, he wrote *The Hula* and earlier this year, Bess Press published his how-to manual *How to Make Your Own Hawaiian Musical Instruments.*

DEDICATION

This is for Bob Schmitt, the state statistician, the Big Daddy of Fax Freex.

This book was designed, typeset and produced by Honolulu Publishing Company, Ltd. Graphic research was conducted by Jerry Hopkins and the production staff of Honolulu Publishing; many graphic materials were drawn from the archives of *Paradise of the Pacific* magazine, with permission from Honolulu Publishing. Chapter title drawings are by Denise Ratliff.

LIBRARY OF CONGRESS CATALOG CARD NO:, 88-72093
ISBN: 0-935848-68-1

CONTENTS

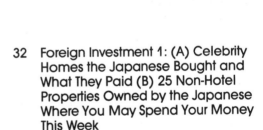

ONLY IN HAWAII

10 Only in Hawaii
11 18 Things You Didn't Know They Taught at the University of Hawaii
12 12 Things We Do Have
13 12 Things We Don't Have
14 5 Superlatives Good Enough for Guinness
15 4 Superlatives That Guinness Overlooked
16 Where the Worst Air Is
17 9 Curious Books About the Romantic South Seas
18 34 Custom Car Plates
20 You Born Year of the Rat or Wot?
21 10 Popular Bumper Stickers
21 10 Icky Truths About the Cockroach
22 10 Reasons to Take the Next Flight Out
23 12 Most Dangerous Intersections
24 How We Stack Up

BUSINESS & MONEY

26 5 Local Products You Have to Wonder About
27 Companies That Begin with Da
28 A Store Is Born . . . Let's Give It a Cute Name
29 15 Categories You Didn't Know Were in the Yellow Pages
30 How Many Readers?
31 So You Wanna Be a Tourist? (Take Your Credit Card)
32 Foreign Investment 1: (A) Celebrity Homes the Japanese Bought and What They Paid (B) 25 Non-Hotel Properties Owned by the Japanese Where You May Spend Your Money This Week
33 Foreign Investment 2: What the Stars Invest In
34 10 Most Popular Cars (By Number of Recent Sales)
35 Where the Jobs Are Gonna Be
36 6 Richest Residents (and Families)
36 How Much You Make?
38 Up from the Poverty Threshold

FOOD

40 2 Shark Recipes
41 The Price of a Glass of Beer
42 Foods Women Couldn't Eat in Ancient Hawaii
43 17 Sashimi Plates and What They Cost
44 9 Most Fattening Plate Lunches
45 7 Ways to Keep Roaches Out of the Kitchen
46 6 Basic Hawaiian Food Groups
46 8 Most Popular Fundraiser Foods
47 12 Local Foods That Even Mainland Haoles Like
48 2 Spam Recipes
48 10 More Ways to Camouflage the Taste of Spam
49 How to Speak Fluent Sushi

CELEBRITIES

52 What They Did Before Getting Famous
53 Celebrity Astrology
58 20 Big Shots with Homes in Hawaii (and Where)
59 15 Movie & TV Locations
60 14 Lefties & Goofy-Foots
61 10 Things Named for Ellison Onizuka
62 12 People Who Actually Live in Waikiki
63 8 Movie Hawaiians
64 13 Hollywood Hula Girls

NATURE

66 7 Pakalolo Songs
67 When the Flowers Bloom
68 7 Mongoose Facts
69 Where the Water Goes
70 Sunniest Neighborhoods
71 Cloudiest Neighborhoods
72 10 Amazing Volcano Fax
73 9 Native Hawaiian Medicines
74 Adopt a Bird or Beast
76 Where the Mammals Are

GEOGRAPHY & HISTORY

80   8 Royal Signatures
82   What Time Is It Here?
83   18 Rules for Prostitutes During World War II
84   10 Things You Didn't Know About Hawaii & World War II
86   20 States with "No" Votes on Statehood
87   If This Is Honolulu, Why Am I Having Dinner at the California Pizza Kitchen?
88   10 Oldest Schools
89   20 Island Names to Broke Da Mout'
90   What Did You Do in the Peace, Daddy?
91   The Hula's Bummest Rap!
92   How the Beaches Got Their Names

SPORTS

94   60 High School Teams & What They're Called
96   41 Olympians Living in Hawaii
98   10 Surfing Landmarks
100   Surf's Up! Twenty Feet and Glassy!
101   12 Celebrity Surfers
102   20 Celebrity Golfers
103   12 Celebrity Runners
104   Other Kine Celebrity Jocks

LOCAL OUT

106   That's Funny, You Don't Look Hawaiian
106   There Is Only 1 Pure Hawaiian at Kam!
107   Inter Racial Marriage
109   8 Mormon Facts
110   Who's Got the Good Jobs? By Ethnic Group
111   Cancer Rates, By Ethnic Group
112   How Many Teenagers? By Ethnic Group
112   Teenage Moms, By Ethnic Group (Ages 12-18)
113   Habla El Tagalog?
114   The High Cost of Dying
115   Where the "Brains" Are (By Neighborhood)
116   20 Most Dangerous Schools
117   Most Arrests, By Ethnic Group
118   16 Miscellaneous Facts
120   How Many Are There?
122   9 Ways to Say "I Love You"

Paradise of the Pacific

▼△▼△▼△▼△▼△▼

ONLY IN HAWAII...

1. ...is bad weather (rain) called a blessing.

2. ...is being late socially acceptable (Hawaiian time).

3. ...do waterfalls fall up, along the Nuuanu Pali on Oahu when the tradewinds are brisk enough to blow the water back up the face of the perpendicular cliffs.

4. ...is it really okay that gasoline is more expensive than anywhere else on the earth—after all, where is there to go?

5. ...does FBI mean Full-Blooded Ilocano.

6. ...do you take off your shoes when you enter the house.

7. ...can you buy "island shells" from the Philippines, drink a local beer (Primo) that's brewed and bottled in California, and eat mahimahi that's imported from Peru.

8. ...do all buses end up at a shopping center, Ala Moana.

9. ...is seaweed a common edible.

10. ...can you call so far on the phone for so little cost; the Big Island operates the largest toll-free calling area in the U.S., 4,038 square miles.

11. ...do we haul out winter clothing when the mercury dips below 70 degrees.

12. ...does summertime mean grocery bags full of mangoes at the office (especially if you work with anyone who lives in Kaimuki).

18 THINGS YOU DIDN'T KNOW THEY TAUGHT AT THE UNIVERSITY OF HAWAII

1. Advanced Reading of Russian Press (Dept. of European Language & Literature)
2. Beginning, Intermediate & Advanced Golf (Physical Education)
3. Gravity (Geology & Geophysics)
4. Women in Revolt (History)
5. Monsoon Meteorology (Meteorology)
6. Solid Waste Management and Control (Engineering)
7. Water Polo (Physical Education)
8. Witches and Witchcraft (Religion)
9. Love, Sex and Religion (Religion)
10. Plant Nutrition and Water Relations (Botany)
11. Puppetry (Drama and Theatre)
12. Practical German for Use in Hawaii (Ethnic Studies)
13. Bowling (Physical Education)
14. Three-Dimensional Fiber Forms (Art)
15. The Personal Journal (Psychology)
16. Prestressed Concrete (Engineering)
17. Ocean Waves I and II (Oceanography)
18. Pineapple Culture (Tropical Agriculture)

Source: *University of Hawaii catalog*

Paradise of the Pacific

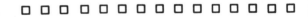

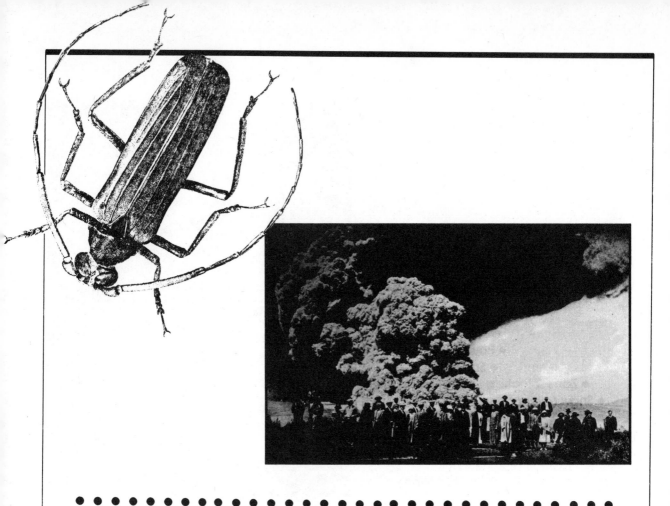

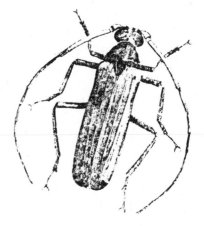

12 THINGS WE DO HAVE
1. Ukus
2. Kona winds
3. Tsunamis
4. Destructive lava flows
5. Portuguese Men-of-War
6. Stinging limu
7. Quarantine for our beloved pets
8. Earthquakes
9. Vog
10. Kiawe thorns
11. Cockroaches
12. Haole rot

Camera Hawaii

o o o o o o o o o o o o o o o o o o o o o o o o o

12 THINGS WE DON'T HAVE

1. Billboards
2. Rabies
3. Motor homes
4. The death sentence
5. Pay toilets
6. Snakes
7. Zone telephone billing for local calls
8. Snow (except on Mauna Kea, Mauna Loa, and Haleakala)
9. Presidential primaries
10. State police
11. Daylight Savings Time
12. Plane hijackers

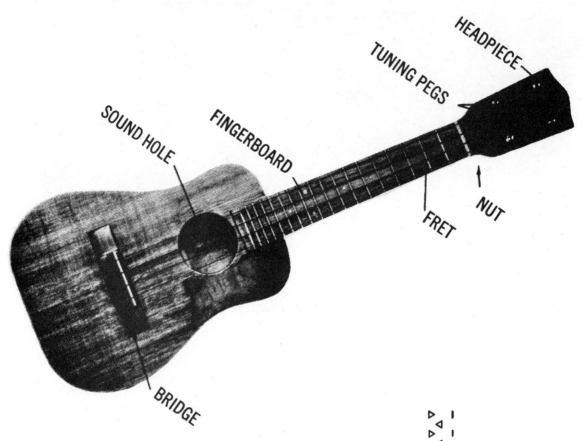

HEADPIECE

TUNING PEGS

FINGERBOARD

SOUND HOLE

NUT

FRET

BRIDGE

5 SUPERLATIVES GOOD ENOUGH FOR GUINNESS

The Book of World Records, that is . . .

1. The biggest barbecue served 15,000, who consumed 43,386 huli-huli chicken halves at Iolani School on Jan. 31, 1981 under the direction of Ernie Morgado

2. Waialeale on Kauai has the most rainy days—up to 350 a year

3. The rarest bird is the o'oa'a; only two have been sighted in any recent year, not far from where it rains so much on Kauai

4. The American Music Conference announced in 1977 that the easiest instrument to play is the ukulele

5. The highest sea cliffs in the world are on the north coast of east Molokai, near Umilehi Point, which descend 3,300 feet to the sea at an average gradient of more than 55 degrees

Source: *Guinness Book of World Records, 1985*

■ ■ ■ ■ ■ ■ ■

4 SUPERLATIVES THAT GUINNESS OVERLOOKED

1. The 100th/442 Regimental Combat Team was the most decorated unit in World War II; at maximum strength there were 4,500 men, yet the unit earned more than 18,400 individual decorations, including 9,486 Purple Hearts and 5,200 Bronze Stars.

2. Salevaa Fuauli Atisanoe, alias Konishiki, is the world's heaviest sumo wrestler, at 527 pounds.

3. Hawaiian Electric Industries Inc. built the world's largest and most powerful windmill in the world, a 3,200-kilowatt turbine that stands 360 feet from base to blade tip in the hills behind Kahuku; it generates enough electricity for 1,140 homes and saves about 13,500 barrels of fuel oil per year; each blade weighs 159 tons and can withstand winds up to 125 mph.

4. Hawaii is the fastest growing place; the 1950 eruption that destroyed the town of Kapoho on the Big Island added almost 500 acres of new land to the shoreline at Cape Kumukahi, and the current eruption and flow near Kalapana has added another 50-plus acres.

WHERE THE WORST AIR IS

Carbon monoxide concentration, parts per million—compared with the Royal Hawaiian Hotel lobby at 0.3 ppm

Ala Moana Center

1. Bank of Hawaii drive-up area 105.0
2. Bus stop, covered parking area ... 82.0
3. Post office 58.7
4. Covered parking area
   (north side of center 32.3
5. Sears automotive garage 30.7

Waikiki

1. Sheraton Hotel parking garage ... 20.0
2. Ala Wai Blvd 9.7
3. Waikiki Theater parking garage 9.0
4. Kapiolani Park jogging path
   next to Paki Ave 7.7
5. Waikiki Shopping Plaza
   (first floor mall) 6.8

Downtown

1. Straub Hospital parking garage .. 15.5
2. Jake's Restaurant 5.2
3. Queen's Hospital
   lobby/cafeteria 4.8
4. Central Pacific Bank 4.3
5. State Capitol (first & fourth floors) .. 4.2

Source: *A Seasonal Study of Personal Exposure to Carbon Monoxide in Indoor and Outdoor Microenvironments of Honolulu by Peter Flachsbart & Dennis Brown, University of Hawaii at Manoa, 1986*

9 CURIOUS BOOKS ABOUT
THE ROMANTIC SOUTH SEAS

1. *The Sweet Potato & Oceania* by D.E. Yen, 383 pages from the Bishop Museum Press, 1974

2. *Handbook of Hawaiian Weeds*, edited by E.L. Haselword & G.G. Motter, University of Hawaii Press, 1983; this one a staggering 491 pages!

3. *Environmental Factors Affecting Stress and Mortality of the Hawaiian Anchovy in Captivity* by Jeanette Whipple Struhraker, Wayne J. Baldwin & Garth I. Murphy, University of Hawaii Sea Grant Program, 1975, and to make up for the length of the title, only 124 pages long.

4. *The Australian Ugliness* by Robin Boyd, Penguin Books, 1980. (A book about the architecture, mostly.)

5. *Dog & Man in the Ancient Pacific* by Margaret Titcomb with Mary Kawena Pukui, Bishop Museum Press, 1969; only 91 pages, but it includes instructions for fattening, killing and cooking the pets, should you really want to know.

6. *The Grasses of Fiji* by J.W. Parham, Colony of Fiji, Government Press, 1955.

7. *Headhunting in the Solomon Islands Around the Coral Sea,* a personal reminscense by Caroline Mytinger, MacMillan, 1942.

8. *The Camel in Australia* by Tom L. McKnight, Melbourne University Press, 1969; a 154-page history.

9. *Filth-inhabiting Flies of Guam* by George Bohart and Linsley Gressit, Bernice P. Bishop Museum Bulletin No. 204, 1951.

Source: *All are available at the Hawaii State Library, Downtown branch*

34 CUSTOM CAR PLATES
Who Owns 'Em and
Why They Say What They Say

1. LUCILLE—Frank Delima, for the song of the same name
2. OV LOV—Richard Quinn; see it in your rear view mirror and it spells the kind of car it's on
3. HW JR—Henry Walker Jr., the Amfac president, on his red Ferrari
4. HAL—Jack Magoon, head of Hawaiian Air Lines (HAL)
5. NOHE—Nohelani Cypriano, the singer, on her Jaguar XKE
6, 7 & 8. SURVEY, SIRVEY and SURVAY—Mike Doyle Ltd., marine surveyors
9. KEKUA—Kekua Fernandez, the singer
10. MOVIES—Consolidated Theaters, the largest theater chain in Hawaii; it's a Morris Minor with a Rolls Royce grill
11. PRRRRR—Elissa Josephson, because she's in PR (public relations) and has cats

12. ADS—Allen Starr of Starr, Seigle, McCombs ad agency; his daughter says it stands for Allen 'Daddy' Starr
13. HEARTS—Dr. Michael Dang, a cardiologist
14. WIN WIN—Carol Maero, who runs New Age workshops and seminars, where everyone wins
15. TIHATI—on Tihati's Lincoln (what a surprise)
16. BURL—Burl Burlingame, the writer for the Star-Bulletin
17. BREWER—Yvonne Brewer, who has nothing to do with beer
18. I FISH—Yvonne Brewer's husband, William, who is a fly fisherman
19. SLICK—Ursula Fisher, who drives a black Porsche; it's her nickname (and no smart remarks)

20 & 21. NUTS and BOLTS—Irene and Bill Hayes, who own Hawaii Nut & Bolt Inc.

22. FASI—on the Mayor's van, painted to look like TheBus

23. DIABLO—Sgt. Maj. Elliott Harvey III, whose Navy squadron is called the Fighting Red Devils

24. PRIMO—Bob Nichols, owner of Primo Builders

25. BEAUTY—Jim Granzow, who owns Jimmy's, a beauty salon in Kilohana Square

26. ALOE—Duane Alamoureaux, who owns Waikiki Aloe, a tanning and skin care company

27. N-SHAPE—DeDe Soares of DeDe's N-SHAPE Studios in Kaimuki

28. KITES—Robert Loera, who owns Kites Fantasy, the kite store makai of Kapiolani Park

29. TIGER—Julia Sohn, who says she isn't a tiger but was born during the year of

30. THE CAR—Fred Livingston, who owns Matteo's; he says it's a joke between him and the valets at his restaurant, whom he is always telling, "Get the car…"

31. GDA—Gloria Damron of Gloria Damron & Associates, the wildly successful Realty

32. GDA 1—Irene Small, who was given the plate when she was Gloria's No. 1 salesperson

33. LA LAW—William Fenton Sink, a lawyer, who isn't even from L.A., but San Diego

34. TOP GUM—John Ebert, a dentist who specializes in periodontal (gum) surgery

Sources: *the drivers themselves*

YOU BORN YEAR OF THE RAT
OR WHAT?

Year of the Rat
1888
1900
1912
1924
1936
1948
1960
1972
1984

Year of the Ox
1889
1901
1913
1925
1937
1949
1961
1973
1985

Year of the Tiger
1890
1902
1914
1926
1938
1950
1962
1974
1986

Year of the Rabbit
1891
1903
1915
1927
1939
1951
1963
1975
1987

Year of the Dragon
1892
1904
1916
1928
1940
1952
1964
1976

Year of the Serpent
1893
1905
1917
1929
1941
1953
1965
1977

Year of the Horse
1894
1906
1918
1930
1942
1954
1966
1978

Year of the Ram
1895
1907
1919
1931
1943
1955
1967
1979

Year of the Monkey
1896
1908
1920
1932
1944
1956
1968
1980

Year of the Rooster
1897
1909
1921
1933
1945
1957
1969
1981

Year of the Dog
1898
1910
1922
1934
1946
1958
1970
1982

Year of the Boar
1899
1911
1923
1935
1947
1959
1971
1983

10 POPULAR
BUMPER STICKERS

1. I'd Rather Be Riding a Mule on Molokai
2. Divers Do It Deeper
3. Body Surfers Do It Wetter
4. I'd Rather Be Doing It Deeper
5. Divers Do It with Mules
6. Mules Do It with Body Surfers
9. I'd Rather Be Doing It with a Mule on Molokai
10. Wet Mules on Drugs

• • • • • • • •

10 ICKY TRUTHS ABOUT
THE COCKROACH

1. Every mama roach can give birth to tens of thousands of offspring a year.
2. They can go for weeks without food or water and can live off the glue on the back of wallpaper for up to five months.
3. Researchers at Emory University in Atlanta studied cockroaches on treadmills, because they say the cockroach's skeletal musculature is similar in design to the human's.
4. Roaches have footpads like our tongues, so that they can taste what they're walking on.
5. The cockroach can carry more than 20 diseases, including salmonella, infectious hepatitis, cholera, dysentery, leprosy, typhoid and plague.
6. They also may carry a variety of worm eggs—hookworm, roundworm, pinworm, tapeworm and whipworm.
7. The life span of a cockroach can be as long as four or five years.
8. A cockroach can live several weeks with its head cut off.
9. There are 18 varieties in Hawaii. The biggest is the American, measuring 1½ inches from nose to tail (not counting the antenna). They're also good fliers.
10. Roaches are not all bad. They figure in the food cycles of many lizards and birds and according to some entymologists, they may some day be a source of protein for humans.

10 REASONS TO TAKE THE NEXT FLIGHT OUT

1. One out of every 45 people in the state has a real estate license.
2. When the polar caps melt, thanks to the "greenhouse effect" which will come due to a loss of ozone in the atmosphere, the oceans will rise and Waikiki will be underwater—at least ankle-deep in the third floor of most hotels. Much of the rest of Hawaii will be underwater, too.
3. Hawaii spends less money per capita on mental health than any other state.
4. We're No. 1 in energy costs: gasoline costs $1.08 a gallon compared to 83 cents nationally; residential electricity is 11.3 cents per kilowatt hour compared to 6.8 cents nationwide; and gas for residential use costs $17.94 per million BTUs, a figure three times greater than the national average of $5.88.
5. We have the most expensive homes, with recent resales averaging $198,400.
6. And...we have the most expensive groceries, costing $65.83 for a "market basket" duplicated in 17 cities; average cost nationally was $51.98.
7. Many major sporting events are broadcast on satellite delay.
8. Hawaii ranks 47th in votes cast as a percentage of voting age population.
9. Hawaii has "America's longest lived political machine"—28 years old and still counting, from John Burns through George Ariyoshi to John Waihee.
10. The incidence of major crime is increasing—with murder up 27.8 percent over the previous year; robberies up 7.1 percent; aggravated assault, 30.9 percent; burglary up 18.4 percent; larceny-theft up 7.1 percent; and auto theft, up 18 percent.

Source: (1) Honolulu Board of Realtors; (2) Dr. Lorenz Magaard, chairman, University of Hawaii Dept. of Oceanography; (3) Public Citizen Health Research Group, a private, nonprofit organization associated with Ralph Nader; (4 & 8) Research & Economic Analysis Division, Dept. of Business & Economic Development; (5) National Board of Realtors; (6) Tampa, Fla. Tribune; (9) Dictionary of American Politics; (10) Honolulu Police Dept., Annual Statistical Report.

Brett Uprichard

● ● ● ● ● ● ● ● ● ● ● ●

12 MOST DANGEROUS INTERSECTIONS

1. Kapiolani Blvd. & Keeaumoku St.
2. Kapiolani and Piikoi St.
3. King St. and Waiakamilo Rd.
4. Kaiulani Ave. and Kuhio Ave.
5. Kapiolani and Pumehana St.
6. King and Punahou Sts.
7. Kapiolani and Kaheka St.
8. Kamehameha Hwy. and Center Dr.
9. Nimitz Hwy. and Lagoon Dr.
10. Castle Junction
11. Likelike Hwy. and School St.
12. Pali Hwy. and Old Pali Rd.

Source: *American Automobile Assn., based on number of accidents and related injuries, amount of traffic and how long the intersection has had a high number of accidents and injuries; majority of accidents were rear end collisions or caused by drivers making illegal left turns.*

Look what they've done to my song, ma! There's a Blue Hawaii Restaurant on King Street, a Sweet Leilani Flowers on Nuuanu Avenue and an Aloha 'Oe Drive in Maunawili.

HOW WE STACK UP

Brett Uprichard

How Hawaii ranks with the other 49 states

1. 1st in life expectancy
2. Last in deaths (per 1,000 population) due to diseases of the heart, 47th in deaths caused by cancer
3. 6th in family living costs
4. 11th in public school pupil-teacher ratio
5. 8th in percent of business establishments foreign owned
6. Highest annual average daily mean temperature (77 degrees F.)
7. 19th in crime rate (per 100,000 population)
8. 7th windiest
9. 2nd highest wages in construction, 21st highest in retail trade
10. 5th highest median family income ($22,750, compared to a national average of $19,917)
11. 5th highest amount of life insurance in force per family
12. 9th in beer consumption per capita (41 gallons)
13. 39th in business failures
14. 5th in the per capita state appropriations for state arts agencies
15. 17th in number of prisoners per 100,000 population
16. 2nd in number of eradicated marijuana plants
17. 18th in annual average teacher's salary

18. 10th in state and local expenditures per capita
19. 38th in number of marriages per 1,000 population
20. 41st in the number of divorces

Source: *State of Hawaii Data Book, Dept. of Business and Economic Development, 1987*

Listed in the Oahu telephone directory you will find 18 Sins, no Virtues, 29 Goods and only one Bad.

■ ■ ■ ■ ■ ■

5 LOCAL PRODUCTS YOU HAVE TO WONDER ABOUT

1. *Frozen Poi Yogurt:*
an invention of Michael Chock, owner of Columbo's Frozen Yogurt Shop in Downtown Honolulu, a shop that no longer exists.

2. *Sole Suckers:*
sandals that stuck to your feet so there were no straps, from Charlie Carr of Cheap Charlie's Inc., another firm that didn't make it.

3. *Plastic ti leaf skirts:*
for dancers on the mainland where there is no ti, or where the leaves won't stay fresh for the duration of the tour; available at Hula Supply on King Street.

4. *Shark Jerky:*
from Charles Herzog III, who already has successfully marketed the most popular brand of surfboard wax, Sex Wax; the price is about the same as for beef jerky and offers the buyer a chance to "bite back"; Waianae's Rell Sunn was the local spokesperson.

5. *Scratch-and-sniff greeting cards:*
with coconut and banana smells, available at Second Image stores.

← Da Boss...

16 COMPANIES THAT BEGIN WITH DA

Oahu
1. Da Illustrator (sign painter), Kalihi
2. Da Lunch Wagon, Kakaako
3. Da Balloon Shop, Pearl City
4. Da Donut Shop, Nimitz Highway
5. Da Smoke House (restaurant), Waikiki
6. Da Winery, Kakaako
7. Da Mix Plate and Chop Suey Clothing Co., Kaimuki

Big Island
1. Da Store, Pahoa
2. Da Warrior Charter Fishing, Kailua-Kona
3. Da Poi Bowl, Keaau

Maui
1. Da Handyman, Makawao
2. Da-Kine Kitchen, Haiku
3. Da Nut Hut Inc., Lahaina

Molokai
1. Da Cowboy Shop, Kaunakakai

Kauai
1. Da Booze Shop, Waimea
2. Da Latest Kine, Waimea

Source: *Telephone & various business directories*

Paradise of the Pacific

A STORE IS BORN—LET'S GIVE IT A CUTE NAME

1. Aunty Pasto's, an Italian restaurant on Beretania
2. The Garden of Eatin', another restaurant, on Farrington Hwy.
3. The Old Volks Home, a car repair shop in Kailua
4. Peter Pawn, hock shop on Keeaumoku Street
5. Phil's Gold, Downtown
6. Shear Madness, beauty parlor, Moiliili
7. Hawaiian Hairlines, same kine shop, Kailua-Kona
8. Slow Poke, fresh fish, Kahala and Kaneohe
9. Apparels of Pauline, clothing, Lahaina
10. Hawaiian Eye Land, optician, Waikiki and McCully
11. Monkey Bar, famous tavern in Pearl City
12. Rabbit Transit, messenger service, Downtown
13. For Shore, beach supplies, Haleiwa
14. Thirst Aid Station, juice bar, Ala Moana Center
15. Hair Apparent, pet groomer in Honolulu
16. Boutiki, gift shop, Pearl Harbor
17. Hair Waves, beauty salon, Kapiolani district
18. Look a Head, another in the same neighborhood
19. Manestreet, still another, in Moiliili
20. A Bear in Mind, stuffed animals on Piikoi
21. Ballooney Tunes, balloons and party items, Kakaako
22. Lickety Split, ice cream, Hawaii Kai
23. High as a Kite, kite store, Lahaina and Kihei
24. Tree Wise Men, tree-trimmers, Kahala

Honolulu Publishing Co., Ltd.

● ● ● ● ● ● ● ● ● ● ● ● ●

15 CATEGORIES YOU DIDN'T KNOW WERE IN THE YELLOW PAGES

1. Artificial Breasts
2. Fur Dyers & Cleaners
3. Genealogy Supplies
4. Coin & Bill Counting and Wrapping
5. Ice Sculptors
6. Pet Exercising Equipment
7. Cement Colors & Hardeners
8. Ozone Equipment
9. Critical Path Scheduling
10. Paper Hats
11. Robots
12. Dirt
13. Boat Upholsterers
14. Beds, Disappearing
15. Cremation Services, Prearranged

Source: *Telephone books, all islands*

HOW MANY READERS?
Circulation of selected publications

1.	MidWeek	266,000
2.	Star-Bulletin & Advertiser (Sunday)	199,700
3.	Hawaii Cable Guide	198,000
4.	Sun Press (all editions)	126,000
5.	Star Bulletin	99,700
6.	This Week (all editions)	96,500
	Oahu	40,000
	Maui	24,500
	Big Island	16,500
	Kauai	15,500
7.	Honolulu Advertiser	88,500
8.	Waikiki Beach Press (Eng. & Japanese)	80,000
	English edition	45,000
	Japanese edition	35,000
9.	Ka Wai Ola O Oha (Office of Haw'n. Affairs)	45,000
10.	Honolulu Magazine	35,000
11.	Hawaii Tribune-Herald (Hilo)	20,000
12.	Ka Leo (University of Hawaii, Manoa)	20,000
13.	Kauai Times	18,000
14.	Maui News	15,500
15.	Downtown Planet	15,000
16.	Hawaii Investor Magazine	13,500
17.	RSVP	12,000
18.	Hawaii Business	10,800
19.	Hawaii Hochi	10,000
20.	Honolulu Club magazine	10,000
21.	Garden Island (Kauai)	9,500
22.	Historic Hawai'i News (Historic Hawaii Foundation)	8,000
23.	W. Hawaii Today (Big Island)	7,700
24.	Hawaii Catholic Herald	7,000

Sources: *the publications*

SO YOU WANNA BE A TOURIST?
(Take Your Credit Card)

1. HOTEL ROOM (Aug. rates)
   Waikiki, on the beach $123
   Waikiki, off the beach 53
   West Maui 159
   Hilo 43
   Westin Kauai, courtyard 180
      beachfront 285

2. FERRARI: By the day, depending
   on the model and
   rental agency ...... $229 to $349.95

3. DON HO:
   Cocktail show $24
   Dinner cruise & show 39.95

4. WATER SPORTS:
   Jet ski .... $20/½ hr.; $35/hr.
   Windsurfing (3-hr lesson) $30
   Snorkeling,
      Hanauma Bay .... $5 to $7
   Waterskiing (for 2) ...... $35/½ hr.
          (for 4) .... $65/hr.
   Parasailing $39.50/person
   Outrigger wave-riding
      (3 waves) $8/person

LIVE AT FIVE...
YOUR PLACE OR MINE?

Peel-a-Grams are rated G, PG, R, X, XX and XXX. "G" gets you a female in a 1-pc. body suit, a male in boxer shorts, for $57.20. Triple-X is an all-nude male or female in a 20-min. floor show, for $104.

Source: *Peel-a-Gram*

FOREIGN INVESTMENT: I

(A) Celebrity Homes the Japanese Bought—and What They Paid

1. Kaiser Estate ($42.5 million)
2. Coconut Island ($8.5 million)
3. Casa Blanca del Mar, Kahala ($21 million)
4. Cec Heftel, Kahala ($3.2 million)
5. Maurice Sullivan, Aina Haina ($5.8 million)
6. Rothschild Estate, Kailua ($2.5 million)
7. Bishop John Scanlan, Diamond Head ($5 million)
8. Allan Carr, Diamond Head ($9.5 million in a 5-home package)
9. Clare Booth Luce, Kahala ($3.6 million)
10. Essam Khashoggi, Kahala ($19.2 million)

(B) 25 Non-Hotel Properties Owned by the Japanese Where You May Spend Your Money This Week

1. Ala Moana Shopping Center
2. Koko Marina Shopping Center
3. Gem
4. Canlis Restaurant
5. Love's Bakery
6. Pioneer Plaza
7. Amfac Center
8. Hualalai Center (Kailua-Kona)
9. Senor Popo's
10. Columbia Inn
11. Ala Moana Building
12. Ala Moana Pacific Building
13. Holiday Mart
14. Pioneer Inn (Lahaina)
15. Yacht Harbor Restaurant
16. Wasa Electrical Services
17. Foremost Dairies
18. Hawaii Kai Golf Course
19. Mililani Shopping Center
20. Mililani Golf Course
21. Shirokiya
22. Diamond Head Market
23. Eaton Square
24. El Pollo Loco
25. Burger King

■ ■ ■ ■ ■ ■ ■ ■

FOREIGN INVESTMENT: 2

What the Stars Invest In

1. TOM SELLECK and LARRY MANETTI are among the investors in Black Orchid, a restaurant at Restaurant Row

2. JACK LORD has a big chunk of the Kapalua Bay Hotel

3. DOLLY PARTON is co-owner of the Hawaii Kai restaurant, Dockside Plantation

4. TOM CRUISE and STEVEN SPIELBERG are investors in the Hard Rock Cafe in Waikiki

5. CHARO owns and operates a restaurant, Charo's, at Haena, Kauai

6. JIM NABORS has a macadamia nut farm near Hana, Maui

7. ROGER MOSLEY has a disco in Pearl City, Reni's, and a hair salon in Wahiawa; his corporation is called Black Inc.

8. OLIVIA NEWTON-JOHN owns Koala Blue, the boutique at Kahala Mall

9. HUEY LEWIS is an investor in Sam's Beachside Grill on Front Street in Lahaina, Maui

10. GEORGE BENSON owns and operates Lahaina Sound, a recording studio

11. JANE SEYMOUR and DEAN PITCHFORD (who wrote the song "Fame") put money into the California Pizza Kitchen, in Kahala

12. KAY STARR, with her husband Woody Gunther, is proprietor of the Kreiss Collection and Terra Firma Tiles

13. DIONNE WARWICK is the principal and partner of International Design Network Inc., an interior design, real estate development and marketing company

Honolulu Publishing Co., Ltd.

14. PETER UEBERROTH has a piece of Mungy Inc., which owns the Tony Roma franchise in Hawaii

15. WALLY AMOS still has an interest in his chocolate chip cookie stores in Waikiki and Pearlridge

16. KENNY ROGERS is a partner with Castle & Cooke on Lanai, in real estate development

10 MOST POPULAR CARS
—BY NUMBER OF RECENT SALES

1. Ford 2,546
2. Toyota 2,348
3. Honda 1,882
4. Chevrolet 1,794
5. Nissan 1,432
6. Dodge 1,296
7. Mazda 753
8. Plymouth 662
9. Buick 635
10. Oldsmobile 602

Source: *Hawaii Automobile Auto Dealers,
Jan.-Apr. 1988*

California Here I Come Dept.

WHERE THE JOBS ARE GONNA BE

Projected occupational demand in 1995

	% Growth	Employ- ment
1. Waiters & Waitresses	45%	17,820
2. Cashiers..............	48%	8,940
3. Restaurant cooks	51%	5,890
4. Kitchen workers	38%	8,470
5. Fast food counter help	38%	7,990
6. Bartenders.............	50%	4,000
7. Accountants & auditors	42%	4,830
8. Guards...............	35%	6,110
9. Dining room & bar help..............	40%	4,930
10. Service supervisors	37%	5,630
11. Registered nurses	36%	6,070
12. Counter attendants	40%	4,250
13. Sales supervisors	30%	8,570
14. Janitors & cleaners	28%	11,590
15. Maids & housekeepers	31%	7,250
16. Restaurant greeters	47%	2,300
17. Lawyers	54%	2,000
18. Miscellaneous administrators	31%	5,560
19. Physicians & surgeons	42%	2,200
20. Bus drivers	44%	2,270

Source: *Hawaii State Occupational Information Coordinating Committee, Dept. of Labor & Industrial Relations, 1988*

HOW MUCH YOU MAKE?
Average Pay Rates
Monthly Rates

Junior typist	$1,103
Clerk-stenographer	1,583
Secretary	1,516
Data entry operator	1,218
Bookkeeper, full-charge	1,865
Engineering, drafting technician	2,049
Hospital attendant	1,171
Staff nurse	2,287

Hourly Rates

Housekeeper	$6.71
Cook, general	8.75
Waiter/waitress	3.87
Laborer (light)	7.40
Carpenter (maintenance)	10.77
Electrician (maintenance)	12.49
Automotive mechanic	11.15
Truck driver (1 ½ to 5 tons)	9.78

Source: *Hawaii Employers Council, 1987*

6 RICHEST RESIDENTS (AND FAMILIES)

1. Barbara Cox Anthony .... $1.8 billion*
2. Harry Weinberg .... $800 million
3. Campbell Family .... $600 million
4. Goldman Family .... $600 million
5. Kelley Family .... $350 million
6. Richard Smart .... $275 million

*In 1986, her wealth was estimated at $1.1 billion, which means she increased her total worth $700 million last year, or about $19 million a day.

Source: *"The 400 Richest People in America," Forbes*

Bob Bonner, former FBI agent in charge of cons in Hawaii for 10 years (including the period when Ron Rewald owned the polo club), says that amongst the international community of con men and scammers, Hawaii is known as the "candy store," because it has the highest per capita gullible population.

There are 40 prostitutes in Chinatown. Half are women.
—Source: *Honolulu Police Department, 1988*

Hawaii was the first place outside California to learn of the discovery of gold in the 1840s and for a long time afterward it was the gold miners' primary source of supplies and the only source of citrus.

No Wonder I Haven't Got the Rent Dept.

UP FROM THE POVERTY THRESHOLD
(Possibly the Most Depressing List in the Book)

Income Category	Family Size			
	1	2	3	4
Poverty Threshold	$ 6,310	$ 8,500	$10,690	$12,880
Very Low Income	12,800	14,600	16,400	18,250
Lower Income	20,450	23,350	26,300	29,200
Median Income	25,562	29,187	32,875	36,500
Gap Group	30,675	35,025	39,450	43,800
	5	6	7	8
Poverty Threshold	$15,070	$17,260	$19,450	$21,640
Very Low Income	19,700	21,150	22,650	24,100
Lower Income	31,050	32,850	34,700	36,500
Median Income	38,812	41,062	43,375	45,625
Gap Group	46,575	49,275	52,050	54,750

Source: *Dept. of Housing & Community Development, City & County of Honolulu (based on federal guidelines)*

2 SHARK RECIPES

□ □ □ □ □ □ □ □ □ □ □ □ □ □ □ □ □ □ □

CRISPY SHARK WITH SWEET-SOUR SAUCE

1 lb. shark, cut in 1½-inch cubes

Batter

¼ C flour	½ C water
¼ C cornstarch	½ t salt

Dip shark cubes into batter and deep fry in oil at 350-degree F.

Sweet-sour sauce

¼ C packed brown sugar	1½ tsp. salt
2 t cornstarch, approximately	1 tsp. sesame oil
3 T lemon juice (or vinegar)	½ C water
1½ tsp. shoyu	1 ginger, 1" length, crushed
½ tsp. MSG (monosodium glutamate)	1 clove garlic, crushed

Boil ingredients until sauce thickens. Taste and add more sugar or salt, as desired. Pour sauce over shark cubes and serve.

SHARK TERIYAKI

1 lb shark meat	1 T oil

Teriyaki sauce

2 T shoyu sauce	1 T cornstarch
1 clove garlic	¼ C water
½ tsp. ginger	2 T sherry
1 T brown sugar	

Cut shark into bite-size pieces. Stir-fry in oil until cooked (flesh will be somewhat white in appearance). Pour the prepared teriyaki sauce over the fish and let stand for 15 minutes or longer depending on the size of the pieces. Reheat. Serve as appetizers.

Source: Ono Hawaiian Shark Recipes, *Univ. of Hawaii Sea Grant College Program, 1977*

THE PRICE OF A GLASS OF BEER

1. Columbia Inn .... $1.25 (Bud)
2. T.G.I. Fridays .... 1.95 (Michelob, Miller Lite)
3. Chart House .... 1.50 (Bud, Coors Light)
4. Host Airport Restaurant ... 2.95 (Bud)
5. Ryan's Parkplace .... 1.25 (Bud, Bud Light, Coors Light)
   1.75 (Henry Weinhardt)
   1.95 (Heineken, Steinlager)
6. Anna Bannana's .... 1.25 (Bud)
   1.50 (Michelob Classic Dark)
   1.75 (Steinlager)
7. Hula's Bar & Lei Stand ..... 1.50 (Bud)
8. Shore Bird Broiler .... 3.00 (Bud)
9. Club Hubba Hubba .... 2.50 (Bud, Miller Lite)
10. House Without a Key ..... 2.50 (Michelob)
11. Elephant & Castle .... 1.75 (Bud, Coors, Miller Lite, Henry Weinhardt)
    2.00 (Steinlager)
12. Hawaii Kai Golf Course ... 1.50 (Bud)
13. Moose McGillycuddy's
    University.................. 1.50 (Bud, Bud Light)
    Waikiki .... 2.25 (Bud, Bud Light)
14. Lolli-Pop Lounge .... 3.00 (Bud, Bud Light)

Sources: *The bartenders, telephone survey, July 1988*

Paradise of the Pacific

FOOD WOMEN COULDN'T EAT IN ANCIENT HAWAII

1. Pork
2. Most bananas
3. Coconuts
4. Ulua
5. Kumu
6. Turtle

Source: *Ethnic Foods of Hawaii by Ann Kondo Corum*

HOW DO YOU KNOW IF IT'S RIPE?

1. Avocado: Stick a toothpick into the stem end; if goes in and out easily, time for make guacamole.
2. Pineapple: Leaves should pull out easily.
3. Watermelon: Snap thumb and finger against side fo melon; if says "pink" at you, no ripe...if says "punk," ready fo' eat.
4. Cantaloupe: Belly button should be somewhat soft, and you should be able to hear the seeds moving around inside.
5. Mango: Good and ripe the day before they fall; use a net and if they plop into the net, they're ripe.

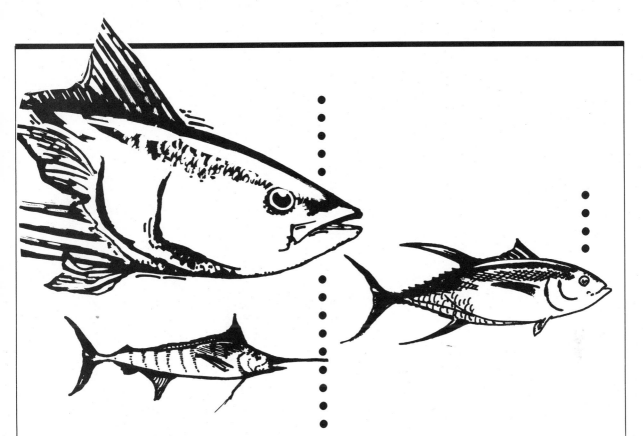

17 SASHIMI PLATES & WHAT THEY COST

1. Pagoda Restaurant $4.95
   (6-7 pieces)
2. Yanagi Sushi 5.95
   (8-10 pieces)
3. Kobe Steak House 6.25
   (7 pieces)
4. Orson's 6.50
   (10 slices)
5. Fisherman's Wharf 6.50
   (9 pieces)
6. Monterey Bay Canners 6.95
   (5 oz.)
7. The Palm Grill 6.95
   (5 oz.)
8. Pearl City Tavern 7.95
   (15 pieces)
9. Tripton's 8.50
   ("enough for two")

10. Third Floor 8.50
    (9 pieces)
11. Surf Room, Royal Hawaiian
    Hotel 8.75
    (5 pieces)
12. John Dominis 8.95
    (8 pieces)
13. The Willows 9.95
    (8 pieces)
14. Orchids 11.75
    (6-7 pieces)
15. Kyo-Ya Restaurant 15.00
    (6 pieces)
16. Michel's 17.00
    (8 pieces; "price changes every day")
17. La Mer 22.00
    by special order

Source: *Telephone survey, April 1988*

□ □ □ □ □ □ □ □ □ □ □ □ □

9 MOST FATTENING PLATE LUNCHES
Counting da Calories Dept.

1. Beef patty 1,200
2. Meatloaf 1,010
3. Loco Moco special 941
4. Fish 730
5. Teriyaki chicken 694
6. Shoyu chicken 644
7. Beef teriyaki 620
8. Stew 523
9. Chili & rice 455

Source: *"Hawaiian Calories"* by
Sandra Kai Jordan, G. Flick, 1984

Paradise of the Pacific

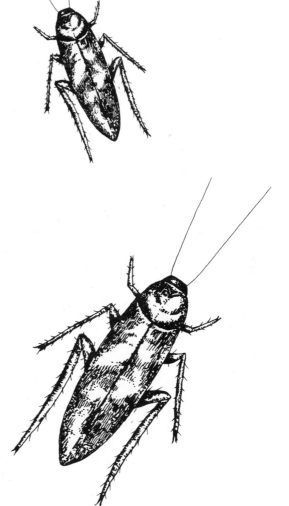

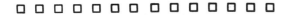

7 WAYS TO KEEP ROACHES OUT OF THE KITCHEN

1. Fill large bowl with cheap wine and place it under the sink. Roaches will drink it, get drunk, fall in and drown. This is not a joke.
2. Sprinkle boric acid powder or borax wherever roaches run.
3. Cut lemon in half, rub around the doorjambs of the house; resident roaches won't leave, but at least no new ones will enter.
4. Put out bay leaves and cucumber peels; will give them a headache at least.
5. Bring in some banana spiders, who eat 10 cockroaches a day; 10 spiders can rid a house of pests in one month.
6. Do not keep paper sacks; roaches love the glue and the darkness.
7. Take all the food into the living room.

Paradise of the Pacific

○ ○ ○ ○ ○ ○ ○ ○ ○

6 BASIC HAWAIIAN FOOD GROUPS

1. **Carbohydrates** (i.e., noodles, pao doce, mochi, musubi, manapua, Maui potato chips, macaroni salad, poi, malasada)
2. **Sugar** (i.e., guava jam, shave ice, haupia, fruit punch)
3. **Salt** (i.e., limu, crack seed, opihi, bagoong)
4. **Grease** (i.e., char siu, pork hash, pork adobo, sweet-sour ribs, Spam, Portuguese sausage)
5. **Fire** (i.e., kim chee, chili peppa water, wasabe, ginger)
6. **Beer**

8 MOST POPULAR FUNDRAISER FOODS

1. Huli Huli chicken
2. Molokai sweet bread
3. Laulau
4. Chili
5. Portuguese sausage
6. Candy
7. Kalua pig
8. Saimin

12 LOCAL FOODS THAT EVEN MAINLAND HAOLES LIKE

1. Saimin—Tastes like a watery noodle soup
2. Shave Ice—They call them "Snow Cones" on the Mainland, where pineapple flavoring is usually yellow instead of blue
3. Mai Tai (and any other drink with Jamaican rum)
4. Maui potato chips
5. Chocolate covered macadamia nuts
6. Potato salad—Mayonnaise and potato, with noodles
7. Macaroni salad—Mayonnaise and noodles, no potatoes
8. Kona coffee
9. Maui lager
10. Mahi burgers
11. Pineapple (when used as decoration for drinks with Jamaican rum)*
12. Almond cookie

*Drinks ordered at Happy Hour or cocktail time with cherries, pineapple, etc., are called Sunset Salads

YOU'LL ENJOY HAWAIIAN BEER

Dim Sum is Chinese for "Little Heart" and Mai Tai is Tahitian for "the very best."

2 SPAM RECIPES

• • • • • • • • • • • • • •

SPAM® AND KIM CHEE CHUN

1 can SPAM®, cut into squares
won bok kim chee, stalks only, rinsed
green onion stalks, cut in 1 inch pieces
celery, cut into thin strips
3-4 eggs
flour
oil for frying

Marinade:

2 Tbsp. shoyu
1 Tbsp. sugar
2 tsp. sesame seeds
1 clove garlic, minced
1 Tbs. oil

Soak SPAM®and vegetables in marinade for about 1 hour then skewer on long cocktail toothpicks, alternating SPAM® between the vegetables. Dredge in some flour and then dip into beaten eggs. Fry in about 2-3 Tsbp. oil over medium heat. Lightly brown on both sides; cool. Remove toothpicks and cut into squares. Serve with vinegar-shoyu sauce.

Vinegar-shoyu sauce:

½ c. Japanese vinegar
2 Tbsp. shoyu
1 clove garlic, minced

SPAM® MUSUBI

Cooked rice
ume
SPAM®
nori

Note: Haoles, you must use Calrose rice, not minute rice

Make musubi as usual, exept make them oblong (SPAM® shape). Slice SPAM® and fry until brown. Cut nori into strips 2-3 inches wide and long enough to go around the musubi. Place a piece of SPAM® on top and wrap nori around it.

Helpful hint making SPAM® shaped musubi from the wisdom of Billy Apele: Save your SPAM® can, pat the rice in the can (be careful...edges of the can are sharp!), and dump it out.

10 MORE WAYS TO CAMOUFLAGE THE TASTE OF SPAM

1. Sweet-Sour Tofu and Spam
2. Spam and Zucchini Omelet
3. Kalua Spam
4. Spam Lumpia
5. Spam Fu Young
6. Spam Quiche
7. Spam Won Ton
8. Sato-Shoyu Spam
9. Spam Saimin
10. Depression Dinner Party Dish

Source: *Hawaii's Spam Cook Book by Ann Kondo Corum*

HOW TO SPEAK FLUENT SUSHI

Japanese	English
Sake	Salmon
Maguro	Tuna
Ika	Squid
Ikura	Salmon roe
Tamago	Omelet stuffed
Toro	Fatty tuna
Ebi	Shrimp
Uni	Sea urchin
Awabi	Abalone
Shimesaba	Mackerel
Mirugai	Trough shell
Hirame	Halibut
Anago	Sea eel
Tako	Octopus
Hamachi	Yellowtail
Kani	Crab
Torigai	Cockle
Tekka & Kappa	Tuna & cucumber rolled in rice with laver

Source: *Yanagi Sushi restaurant*

HAOLE WAY FO' OPEN COCONUTS

Puncture the eyes with an ice pick and drain coconut milk. Bake the coconut in shallow pan at 350 degrees for 45 minutes to one hour, until shell begins to crack. Cool, then tap with a hammer. Shell should almost spring apart.

HOW FO' RIPEN FRUIT FAS'

1. Green bananas: wrap in wet dish towel, store in paper bag.
2. Avocados: store in a paper bag or bury in a bowl of flower.
3. Green fruit: store in perforated plastic bag.

It takes three feet of sugar cane to make one lump of sugar.

At large feasts in the early 1800s, as many as 200 to 400 dogs could be served. Raised as vegetarians, their flesh was considered quite tasty, and healthy.
Source: *Atlas of Hawaii*

HOW FO' GET HAIR OFF KAHUKU CORN

Dampen a paper towel and brush downward on the cob. Every strand should come off.

WHAT THEY DID BEFORE GETTING FAMOUS

1. Wally "Famous" Amos was a record promoter

2. Neil Abercrombie was a parole officer

3. Emme Tomimbang was a model who appeared in a bikini on the front page of Pacific Business News

4. Jay Larrin was a French teacher at Kailua High

5. Reputed crime chieftain (as the dailies always call him) Henry Huihui was an electrician

6. Keo Sananikone, who owns Keo's Thai restaurant, worked in his father's Pepsi Cola franchise in Cambodia; his first job in Hawaii was as a cook at Burger King

7. Bob Longhi, another restaurateur, on Maui, was an insurance salesman

8. Bob Flowers, the plastic surgeon, was a preacher and a bandleader

9. Jim Nabors was a waiter

10. Frank Fasi sold building supplies

11. Larry Price, the radio personality, was coach of the UH football team

12. Another radio personality, Kimo Kahoano, was a knife dancer who opened the show for Danny Kaleikini at the Kahala Hilton

13. Rick Davis, publisher of Aloha magazine, was a stockbroker

14. Connie Conrad, the jeweler, designed tombstones

15. U.S. Rep. Pat Saiki taught school at Kaimuki Intermediate, Kalani High School, and Punahou School

16. Maui Mayor Hannibal Tavares was a cop

17. Jeremy Harris, the Honolulu city manager, was an oceanographer

18. Tom Selleck sold airline tickets for United

19. Jack Lord sold Cadillacs

CELEBRITY ASTROLOGY

Aries (Mar. 21-Apr. 20)

Mar. 27—Arnold Morgado
(Honolulu, 1952)

Apr. 9—Tony Narvaes (Honolulu, 1953)

10—Martin Denny
(New York City, 1911)

11—Charles Marsland
(Honolulu, 1923)

12—Tony Kunimura
(Koloa, Kauai; 1923)

13—Sam King
(Hankow, China; 1916)

19—Dick Jensen (Honolulu, 1943);
James Burns (Honolulu, 1937)

Taurus (Apr. 21-May 20)

Apr. 27—Les Keiter (Seattle, 1919)

28—George Chaplin
(Columbia, S.C.; 1914)

29—David Kahanu (Honolulu, 1935)

May 13—Leigh-Wai Doo
(Honolulu, 1946)
John Bellinger
(Honolulu, 1923)

19—John Waihee
(Honoka'a, Big Island; 1946)
Leina'ala Kalama Heine
(Honolulu, 1940)

Andy Cummings

○ ○ ○ ○ ○ ○ ○ ○ ○ ○ ○ ○ ○ ○ ○ ○

Leo (July 23—Aug.22)

July 31—Donna Kim (Honolulu, 1952)
Iva Kinimaka (Honolulu, 1940)

Aug. 2—Andy Cummings
(Honolulu, 1913)

4—Scott Stone
(Polk Co., Tenn; 1932)
Eddie Kamae (Honolulu, 1927)

8—Ed Kenney (Honolulu, 1933)
Wally Fujiyama
(Honolulu, 1925)

10—Hoakalei Kamau'u
(Honolulu, 1929)

13—Don Ho (Honolulu, 1930)

15—Nona Beamer
(Honolulu, 1923)

20—Bob Gibson, the dentist
(Honolulu, 1927)

21—Ka'upena Wong
(Honolulu, 1929)

Richard Smart and Mom

Paradise of the Pacific

Virgo (Aug.23-Sept.22)

Sept. 2—David Schutter
(Appleton, Wis.; 1940)

4—Marisol Borromeo
(Cebu City, P.I., 1959)

7—Dan Inouye (Honolulu, 1924)

9—Leon Edel (Pittsburgh, 1907)

14—Larry Rivera
(Kekaha, Kauai; 1930)

16—Thomas Hitch
(Booneville, Mo.; 1912)

17—Victor Li (Hong Kong, 1941)

Gemini (May 21-June 21)

May 21—Richard Smart
(Honolulu, 1913)

26—Ilima Piianaia
(Honolulu, 1947)

27—Mary George (Seattle, 1916)

28—Pat Saiki (Hilo, 1930)

June 1—Francis Keala (Honolulu, 1930)

8—Terrance Tom (Honolulu, 1948)

9—Kapono Beamer
(Kamuela, Big Island; 1952)

14—Beverly Noa
(Los Angeles, 1933)
John Henry Felix
(Honolulu, 1930)
29—Mary Bitterman
(San Jose, 1944)

Cancer (June 22-July 22)
June 24—Eaton "Bob" Magoon
(Honolulu, 1922)
26—Neil Abercrombie
(Buffalo, N.Y.; 1938)
July 1—George Akahane
(Honolulu, 1929)
13—Bill Quinn
(Rochester, N.Y.; 1919)
14—Sonny Chillingworth
(Honolulu, 1932)
17—John "Doc" Buyers
(Coatesville, Pa., 1928)
18—Melveen Leed (Honolulu, 1943)
Rod Burgess (Honolulu, 1942)

Libra (Sept. 23-Oct. 22)
Sept. 24—Hannibal Tavares
(Makawao, Maui; 1919)
30—Cec Heftel
(Cook Co., Ill.; 1924)
Oct. 1—Hiram Fong (Honolulu, 1907)
2—Edward Kawananakoa
(San Francisco, 1924)
7—Irmgard Aluli (Lahaina, 1911)
8—Chris Hemmeter
(Washington, D.C.; 1939)
Spark Matsunaga
(Kukuiula, Kauai; 1916)
10—Danny Kaleikini
(Honolulu, 1937)
11—Mary Zanakis
(Los Angeles, 1958)
17—Zulu (Hilo, 1937)
18—Eileen Anderson
(Los Angeles, 1928)

Danny Kaleikini

● ● ● ● ● ● ● ● ● ● ● ● ● ● ● ●

Scorpio (Oct. 23-Nov. 21)
Oct. 24—Welcome Fawcett
(Chicago, 1937)
27—Emme Tomimbang
(Honolulu, 1950)
28—Kenneth Brown
(Honolulu, 1919)
30—Jean Ariyoshi (Wahiawa, 1933)

Nov.   2—Fred Rohlfing (Honolulu, 1928)
     5—Chief Justice of Supreme Court
       Herman Lum
       (Honolulu, 1926)
     9—Lynne Waters (Houston, 1957)
   14—Ben Cayetano
       (Honolulu, 1939)
   18—Judge Martin Pence
       (Sterling, Kan., 1904)
   21—Herbert Matayoshi (Hilo, 1928)

Sagittarius (Nov. 22-Dec. 21)
Nov. 27—William Kaina (S. Kona, 1932)
   28—Kenneth Char, Aloha Airlines
       president (Honolulu, 1921)
Dec.   2—John Magoon, Hawaiian
       Airlines president
       (Honolulu, 1915)
     3—Dante Carpenter
       (Honolulu, 1939)
     5—Mahi Beamer (Honolulu, 1928)
       Steve Cobb (Honolulu, 1942)
     6—Patsy Mink (Paia, Maui; 1927)
       Bob Sevey (Minneapolis, 1927)
   12—Al Harrington
       (Yutuila, Amer. Samoa; 1935)
   14—Marlene Sai (Honolulu, 1941)
   18—John Carroll
       (St. Mary's, Kan.; 1929)

Capricorn (Dec. 22-Jan. 19)
Dec. 22—William Richardson
       (Honolulu, 1919)
   28—Richard Kelley (Honolulu, 1933)
   30—Jack Lord (NYC, 1930)
Jan.   1—Robert Wenkam
       (Oakland, Ca.; 1920)
Jan.   1—Kahauanu Lake
       (Wailuku, Maui; 1932
     9—Fred Hemmings (Honolulu, 1946)
   14—Bob Krauss
       (Plainview, Nebr.; 1924)
   15—Clifford Uwaine (Honolulu, 1951)

■ ■ ■ ■ ■ ■ ■ ■ ■

Aquarius (Jan. 20-Feb. 18)

Jan. 23—Uncle Tommy Kaulukukui
(Honolulu, 1913)

25—Bob Schmitt (Cincinnati, 1922)

Feb. 1—Clarence Lee, graphic designer
(Honolulu, 1935)

Feb. 2—James Michener (1907)
Arthur Lyman (Honolulu, 1932)

3—Sterling Mossman
(Honolulu, 1920)

4—Wayne Nishiki (Honolulu, 1944)

5—Henry Peters (Honolulu, 1941)

10—Andy Anderson (Honolulu, 1930)

14—Terence Knapp (London, 1932)

Pisces (Feb. 19-Mar. 20)

Feb. 21—Buck Buchwach
(Portland, Ore.; 1921)

23—George Mason, publisher,
Pacific Business News,
(Buffalo, NY: 1924)

26—Chinn Ho (Honolulu, 1904)

Mar. 3—Moses Keale
(Puuwai, Niihau, 1938)
Malama Solomon
(Big Island, 1951)

7—Robert Pfeiffer (Suva, Fiji; 1920)
Keith Haugen
(Greenbush, Minn.; 1940)

9—Jerry Byrd (Lima, Ohio; 1920)

11—Judge Simeon Acoba
(Honolulu, 1944)

12—George Ariyoshi
(Honolulu, 1926)

Irmgard Aluli

20 BIG SHOTS WITH HOMES IN HAWAII (AND WHERE)

1. Sylvester Stallone, Hanalei
2. Ferdinand & Imelda Marcos, Makiki (formerly of Aina Haina and Hickam Air Force Base)
3. Kenny Rogers, Aina Haina, with financial interests on Lanai
4. Mike Love (Beach Boys), Princeville
5. Charles Schwab, Kailua-Kona
6. Bette Midler, Hanalei and Kilauea
7. Billie Jean King, Hanalei
8. Charo, Hanalei (has a bar there, too)
9. Darryl Dragon (the Captain of the Captain & Tennile), Kohala Ranch
10. Kareem Abdul-Jabbar, Kilauea
11. Wilt "The Stilt" Chamberlain, Waikiki
12. Bert Dohmen, Portlock
13. Taj Mahal, Lihue
14. Tony Curtis, Hawaii Loa
15. Paul Mitchell, Lanikai
16. Roger Mosely, Waikiki (plus a nightclub in Pearl City and a beauty parlor in Wahiawa)
17. Danny Arnold (TV producer), Kahala
18. Glen Frey (the Eagles), Hanalei
19. Rev. Bob Schuller, Kahala and Haiku
20. Richard Chamberlain, Tantalus

Bette Midler

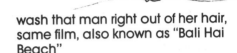

Paradise of the Pacific

15 MOVIE & TV LOCATIONS

1. Universal Studios, 510 18th Ave., Kaimuki/Diamond Head, where most of "Hawaii Five-O" and "Magnum P.I." was filmed

2. Coconut Island, Kaneohe Bay, scene of the opening shots in TV's "Gilligan's Island" and much of *Bird of Paradise* (1951 with Debra Paget)

3. Royal Hawaiian Hotel, used in dozens of shows, including Arthur Godfrey's TV specials and *Gidget Goes Hawaiian* (1961)

4. Iolani Palace, Jack Lord's "office" in "Hawaii Five-O"

5. Waialae Golf Course, Hole No. 1, where Montgomery Clift died in *From Here to Eternity* (1953)

6. Coco Palms Hotel, Wailua, Kauai, home base for Elvis Presley's *Paradise Hawaiian Style* (1966)

7. Slippery Slide, Kilauea, Kauai, created for *South Pacific* (1958)

8. Lumahai Beach, Kauai, where Mitzi Gaynor sang to the world that she'd wash that man right out of her hair, same film, also known as "Bali Hai Beach"

9. House Without a Key, the original beachside bar at the Halekulani Hotel in Waikiki was the inspiration if not the actual site of all the Charlie Chan books and movies; the first novel, called *House Without a Key*, was based roughly on a Honolulu detective who drank there in the 1920s

10. Hanalei Valley, Kauai, King Kong's native habitat (1976)

11. Waimea Bay and the Banzai Pipeline, Oahu, where dozens of surfing films were made

12. Kona Village Resort, Big Island, site of the ill-fated Debbie Reynolds TV show, "Aloha Paradise"

13. Round Top Drive, Oahu, where Elvis serenaded Joan Blackman in *Blue Hawaii* (1961) with Diamond Head in the background

14. The waters off Kauai, *Islands in the Stream*, where George C. Scott and David Hemmings fished (1977)

15. Kauai jungle, opening sequence of Steven Spielberg's *Raiders of the Lost Ark* (1980) and much of *Uncommon Valor* (1983)

Source: *Academy of the Motion Picture Arts & Sciences; the Hollywood Reporter*

14 LEFTIES AND GOOFY-FOOTS

1. Pegge Hopper
2. Kahauanu Lake
3. Roger Mosley
4. Gerry Lopez
5. Charles K.L. Davis
6. Jack Scaff
7. Bla Pahinui
8. Moe Keale
9. Rory Russell
10. Ledward Kaapana
11. Kanoe Cazimero
12. James Michener
13. Richard Pryor
14. Dan Inouye*
15. Sid Fernandez

*He was right-handed before World War II.

10 THINGS NAMED FOR ELLISON ONIZUKA

1. The Air Force renamed the USAF Systems Command headquarters in Sunnyvale, Ca., Onizuka Air Force Station.

2. Funds are now being raised to build a $500,000 "Lt. Col. Ellison S. Onizuka Pavilion and Museum" at Keahole Airport on the Big Island.

3. Hale Pohaku, the mid-level support facility for astronomers on Mauna Kea, was renamed the Onizuka Center for International Astronomy.

4. The Los Angeles City Council voted unanimously to change the name of Weller Street in Little Tokyo to Onizuka Street.

5. A videocassette, "Ellison Onizuka— The Boy, the Man, the Dream," was produced by KHON-TV in Honolulu.

6. The Aloha Council of the Boy Scouts of America created an award in Onizuka's name. (He was an Eagle Scout.)

7. "Ellison S. Onizuka, A Remembrance," a 160-page hardcover book, was published in 1986, proceeds to help pay for the pavilion at Keahole Airport.

8. The Future Farmers of America Club at Konawaena High School on the Big Island dedicated a garden to Onizuka.

9. 26 trees were planted in Onizuka's honor at the Veteran's Memorial Hospital on Kauai, the University of Hawaii and in Hilo.

10. An orchid was named after Onizuka.

Sources: *Star-Bulletin; Pacific Business News*

• • • • • • • • • •

12 PEOPLE WHO ACTUALLY LIVE IN WAIKIKI

At least part of the time...

1. Jay Larrin
2. Don Ho
3. Joe Moore
4. Fred Dailey, president, Hawaii Polo Club
5. Ric Trimillos, head, music department, U of H
6. Peter George, orthodontist, former Olympic gold medal winner for wrestling
7. Kapono Beamer
8. Sol K. Bright Sr.
9. Eddie Sherman, the columnist
10. U.S. Sen. Dan Inouye
11. Wilt "The Stilt" Chamberlain
12. Martin Wolff

Blood Is Thicker than Silver Nitrate Dept.

8 MOVIE HAWAIIANS

1. Delores Del Rio, who is Mexican, played the lead hula dancer in the 1932 version of *Bird of Paradise*

2 & 3: Debra Paget, who is Armenian, and Jeff Chandler, another haole who often played American Indians, played Hawaiians in the remake of *Bird of Paradise*

4. Geraldine Chaplin, Charlie's haole daughter, was 1/4 Hawaiian royalty in *The Hawaiians*

5. Lupe Velez, another Mexican, played the title role of Honolulu Lu in 1942

6. Gilda "The Shimmy Girl" Gray, a haole, played the title role in *Aloma of the South Seas* in 1926

7. George Chakiris, who is Greek, played the Hawaiian male lead in *Diamond Head* in 1963

8. Billy Gilbert, a haole, played a Polynesian with cannibalistic tendencies

HOLLYWOOD & HONOLULU

Linked by the most ENCHANTING VOYAGE *on the seven seas!*

Stevie Nicks, a sometime Maui resident, is the name picked by "Hutch" Hutchinson, the KPOI FM disc jockey, for his daughter and Mike Ebinger, the polo player, for his horse.

Alfred Apaka's son Jeff went to high school in Beverly Hills with Richard Dreyfus, Rob Reiner, and Albert Brooks.

Keep Your Eyes on the Marquee Dept.

13 HOLLYWOOD HULA GIRLS

1. Deborah Walley
(*Gidget Goes Hawaiian*, 1961)
2. Shirley Temple (*Curly Top*, 1935)
3. Jane Russell
(*The Revolt of Mamie Stover*, 1956)
4. Eleanor Powell (*Honolulu*, 1939)
5. Minnie Mouse
(*Hawaiian Holiday*, 1935)
6. Clara Bow (*Hula*, 1927)
7. Dorothy Lamour
(*Road to Singapore*, 1940)
8. Marjorie Main
(*Ma & Pa Kettle at Waikiki*, 1955)
9. Yvette Mimieux
(*Diamond Head*, 1963)
10. Rita Hayworth
(*Sadie Thompson*, 1954)
11. Betty Grable
(*Song of the Islands*, 1942)
12. Jeanette MacDonald
(*Let's Go Native*, 1930, and again in
I Married An Angel, 1942)
13. Marie Osmond
(*Going Coconuts*, 1978)

Source: *The Hula* by Jerry Hopkins

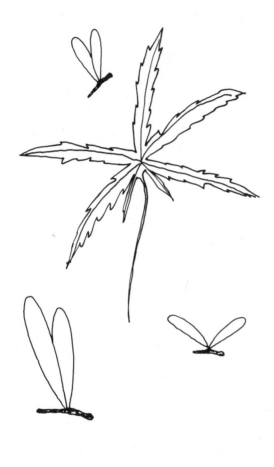

7 PAKALOLO SONGS
(and the groups that recorded them)
1. "Pakalolo" (Makaha Sons of Niihau)
2. "Who Is the Lolo Who Stole My Pakalolo?" (Don Ho)
3. "Cane Fire" (Peter Moon Band)*
4. "Island Love' (Peter Moon Band)
5. "Amazing Little Grass" (Blalahs of Kekaha)
6. "Mea Whirleybird" (Jesse Nakaoka)
7. "Sweet Weoweo" (Sons of Hawaii)

*When the band sings "Save the children!",
the "children" are the pakalolo plants between
the rows of sugar cane.

There are approximately 10,000 different kinds of insects in Hawaii.

A good way to get rid of swarming termites, if you have a pool is to turn on the light at night and the buggahs will fly into the pool and drown; the pool filter should get rid of the little bodies.

The number of snorkelers at Hanauma Bay has increased so rapidly in recent years, there are now serious studies being conducted to determine the effect of two foreign substances in the water— urine and tanning liquids.

WHEN THE FLOWERS BLOOM

It must be summer, I'm up to my okole
in mangoes and shower tree blossoms!

Flower	**Peak months**
1. Red Bougainvillea	Jan.-Mar., June, Nov.-Dec.
2. Red ginger	Jan.-Apr., Dec.
3. Hibiscus	All year
4. Mock orange	June
5. Christmas berry tree	Oct.-Dec.
6. African tulip tree	Jan.-June, Dec.
7. Golden shower tree	June-Aug.
8. Heliconia	June
9. Night-blooming cereus	July-Sept.
10. Jacaranda	Apr.-May
11. Oleander	All year
12. Plumeria	All year
13. Mexican creeper	All year
14. Poinsettia	Jan., Dec.
15. Shrimp plant	All year
16. Umbrella tree	Sept.
17. Lehua haole	Jan.-Mar., Dec.
18. Kou haole	Aug.,-Sept.
19. Royal poinciana (Flame tree)	May-Aug.
20. Golden cup	Jan.-Mar.

Source: *C. Montague Cooke Jr. & Marie C. Neal, Almanac of Hawaiiana, 1969*

▲▼▲ 7 MONGOOSE FACTS

1. The plural is mongooses. Not mongeese.

2. Hunters, bird watchers and poultry farmers hate the mongoose because it eats birds and chickens, but sugar planters love the little furry critter, because it also keeps the rat population down.

3. Actually, the mongoose is not a fussy eater. It also will eat bananas and other fruit, as well as the poisonous buffo toads. (Toads that will make a big dog sick.)

4. The mongoose has a pair of anal glands that supposedly secrete a foul odor like a skunk. This isn't noticeable with one, but when many are together, as when 7,000 were held captive during the 1976 rabies scare, the odor was definitely noticeable.

5. It's illegal to own a mongoose except for scientific experiments.

6. The only two major islands remaining mongoose-free are Lanai and Niihau.

7. The mongoose is classified as a member of the cat family, which makes it more intelligent than your average dog.

WHERE THE WATER GOES

Average consumption of
water resources on Oahu is as follows:

Agriculture (sugar plantations) 50%

Municipal (household) 36%*

Military 8%

Industrial & commercial 6%

*Single family dwelling with family of four uses an
average of 24,000 gallons every two months

Source: *Honolulu Board of Water Supply*

Sometimes the humpback whales take as long as two days to sound and spout and sing their way from Maalaea Bay to Lahaina.

When Hurricane Iwa hit the islands in 1982, the undersea power was so great, the surges picked up a 600-ton mine sweeper that had sunk off the Waianae Coast and moved it so that it was perpendicular to the shoreline instead of parallel. A 30-inch-diameter Pacific Resources pipeline which ran for two miles off Barbers Point was picked up and moved 100 feet sideways by the same storm.

Source: *Andrea Simpson, PRI*

Paradise of the Pacific

SUNNIEST NEIGHBORHOODS

Oahu
1. All the property between Kahala and Sand Island makai of the H-1
2. Kahuku
3. All of Pearl Harbor
4. The entire Waianae coast

Maui
1. Beaches from Hawea Point to Honokowai Point (Napili)
2. Olowalu and five miles of seaside property on either side of this village
3. From Kihei to a point on the rocky lava coastline halfway between Makena and Kipahulu

Big Island
1. Mauna Loa and Mauna Kea down to the 10,000-foot level
2. Upelu Point in North Kohala south to the Kona Village Resort

Kauai
1. Barking Sands south to Kekaha
2. Kaumakani through Hanapepe and Port Allen to Kohe Point
3. Poipu

Molokai
1. Coast Guard Reserve on the northwestern point of the island
2. The southern shoreline from Hale O Lono Harbor past Kaunakakai to Kamiloloa

Source: "Sunshine Maps" prepared by the Dept. of Planning & Economic Development, 1985, rating neighborhoods according to the number of "estimated annual average of calories per square centimeter."

Brett Uprichard

CLOUDIEST NEIGHBORHOODS

Oahu
1. The Koolaus
2. Maunawili
3. Kaneohe
4. Kahaluu north to Hauula
5. The back of Kalihi, Nuuanu, Manoa and Palolo
6. Schofield Barracks Military Reservation

Maui
1. West Maui Mountains
2. Koolau Forest Reserve, Hana Forest Reserve, Kipahulu Forest Reserve, Waihou Forest Reserve, Makawao Forest Reserve, Waihou Spring Reserve
3. Keanae and Wailua
4. Waihee

Big Island
1. Hilo Forest Reserve
2. Kohala Forest Reserve
3. North Kohala coast from Pookalani south to Waipio
4. Glenwood to Mountain View to Kurtistown
5. Kau Forest Reserve

Kauai
1. Waialeale, covering about 50 percent of the island's land mass, including Kokee, most of the Na Pali coast, the back end of the Wailua River, Kapaa Homestead land, and the back of Hanalei Valley

Molokai
1. Molokai Forest Reserve
2. North shore from Kikipua Pt. west almost all the way to Kalaupapa

Source: "Sunshine Maps" prepared by the Dept. of Planning & Economic Development, 1985, rating neighborhoods according to the number of "estimated annual average of calories per square centimeter."

10 EXPLOSIVE VOLCANO FAX

1. The current (1983-88) eruption is the largest of a Hawaii volcano in recorded history.

2. Since January 1983 it has produced 1.2 billion cubic yards of lava—enough to pave a foot-thick, two-lane highway to the moon, or 10 times around the equator.

3. Only about half of the lava reaches the surface.

4. All Hawaii's islands were once located—and were, in fact, formed—where the Big Island is today; they have been "drifting" northwest ever since.

5. At the same time, the islands are sinking from their own weight into a deep, moat-like trench of molten lava; the Big Island is sinking at the rate of 1/10th of an inch annually.

6. In an eruption in 1924, cauliflower clouds were sent boiling four miles above Halemaumau and 14-ton boulders were thrown from the crater.

7. Haleakala is not considered a "dead" volcano, but merely "dormant."

8. The southwestern or makai end of Diamond Head is higher than the opposite end because the trade winds blew much soil and volcanic ash seaward as the crater was being formed.

9. During historic times, Kilauea has been active 62 percent of the time, and Mauna Loa, only 6.2 percent of the time.

10. Lava usually travels between one and 300 yards per hour, but sometimes moves more than 8 to 10 miles an hour.

Source: (1-5) Thomas Wright, scientist in charge, Hawaiian Volcano Observatory; (6) National Park Service publication; (7, 9 & 10) Atlas of Hawaii

□ □ □ □ □ □ □

The tentacles of the Portuguese Man of War, or *physalia utriculus*, are coated with thousands of microscopic cysts, each one of which snaps out a stinging barb which injects a venom into you.
—Source: Harry Arnold Jr., Editor Emeritus, Hawaii Medical Journal

□ □ □ □ □ □ □ □ □ □ □ □ □ □ □ □ □

Scoop up a handful of sand and you're holding about 10,000 grains.

Paradise of the Pacific

9 NATIVE HAWAIIAN MEDICINES

1. **Kukui nut**—Eaten raw, for constipation
2. **Guava**—Young leaf buds chewed and swallowed, for diarrhea
3. **Wild ginger**—Grind the roots, add water and strain; drink clear liquid for stomach ache
4. **Banana**—Juice or sap from cut flower bud treats coated tongue from stomach trouble
5. **Native cotton**—Flowers partly dried and eaten, for stomach cramps
6. **Aloe**—Sap or juice for insect bites, sunburn, athlete's foot and arthritis
7. **Breadfruit**—Sap for cuts, scratches, skin diseases, scaly or cracked skin, sores about the mouth
8. **Ilima**—Another good laxative; chew the mild & tasty flowers
9. **Sugar cane**—Makes bad-tasting medicine taste better

Source: *Native Plants Used as Medicine in Hawaii* *by Beatrice H. Krauss*

How much is that tiger in the window dept.?

ADOPT A BIRD OR BEAST

Agree to pay the specified amount below and you get your name on one of the adoptive "parents recognition posts" in the zoo...an official certificate of adoption with your name and the name of the animal you have selected...a fact sheet on your animal... an "I adopted at the Zoo" bumper sticker...and an invitation to the Honolulu Zoo Hui's annual party.

$15
Domestic Rabbit
Pony
Turkey
African bullfrog
Leghorn chicken
Parachute gecko
Mongoose
Nene
Mexican orange-knee tarantula

$25
Chinese emperor newt
Japanese fire-bellied newt
Hawaiian pig
Spider monkey
Cattle egret
Red-footed booby
Chuckwalla
Hawaiian wild sheep

$50
Gray kangaroo
Wallaby
Great frigate bird
Blue-tongued skink
Ceylon junglefowl
Axis deer
Raven

$100
White stork
American bison
Llama
American alligator
Green iguana
Major Mitchell's cockatoo
Water buffalo
Zebra

Paradise of the Pacific

$250
Ostrich
Chimpanzee
Cougar
Galapagos turtle
Dromedary camel
Reticulated giraffe
Burmese python
Giant anteater

$500
African lion
Bengal lion
Common hippopotamus
Square-lipped rhinoceros

$1,000
Asian elephant
Entire giraffe herd
Entire kangaroo troop

Source: *Honolulu Zoo Hui*

o o o o o o o o o o o o o o o

WHERE THE MAMMALS ARE
Besides humans, you will find the following wild and feral mammals on the following islands:

On all 8 major islands
1. Cat
2. Mouse
3. Norway rat
4. Polynesian rat
5. Roof rat

On Oahu
1. Bat
2. Axis deer
3. Dog
4. Goat
5. Mongoose
6. Pig
7. Rabbit (Manana Is.)
8. Wallaby (Kalihi Valley)

On Maui
1. Bat
2. Axis deer
3. Dog
4. Goat
5. Mongoose
6. Pig

On the Big Island
1. Bat
2. Cattle
3. Dog
4. Donkey
5. Goat
6. Mongoose
7. Mouflon
8. Pig
9. Sheep

On Molokai
1. Cattle
2. Axis deer
3. Dog
4. Goat
5. Mongoose
6. Pig

Camera Hawaii

On Kauai
1. Bat
2. Cattle
3. Mule deer
4. Dog
5. Goat
6. Horse
7. Pig

On Lanai
1. Pronghorn antelope
2. Axis deer
3. Dog
4. Goat
5. Mouflon

On Niihau
1. Pig
2. Rabbit (Lehua Is.)

On Kahoolawe
1. Goat

In Hawaiian waters
20 species of whales & dolphins
Source: State Dept. of Health

△ △ △ △

The American Golden Plover (or Kolea) migrates to and from Hawaii and Alaska, a distance of more than 2,000 miles; leaves here in May, returns in August.
Source: *Hawaii Audubon Society*

The bufo's tongue is hinged at the front and can be flicked out like a whiplash after beetles, moths, army worms, cockroaches, centipedes, wasps, flies, caterpillars, termites and other undesirables.

△ △ △ △ △ △ △ △ △ △ △ △ △ △ △

The rat was not eaten in Hawaii, as it was in New Zealand, but it was used in a formalized contest or sport in which rats were placed in an arena and shot with bows and arrows. This pastime is authenticated only for Hawaii.
Source: *Atlas of Hawaii*

The *aredola ibis*, or cattle egret, comes from north and west Africa, where there are flocks of 5,000. When they settle in for the night on their favorite trees, the branches bend to the ground and it looks like the trees are covered with snow.
Source: *Joe Kimmins, Education Director, Honolulu Zoo*

EIGHT ROYAL SIGNATURES

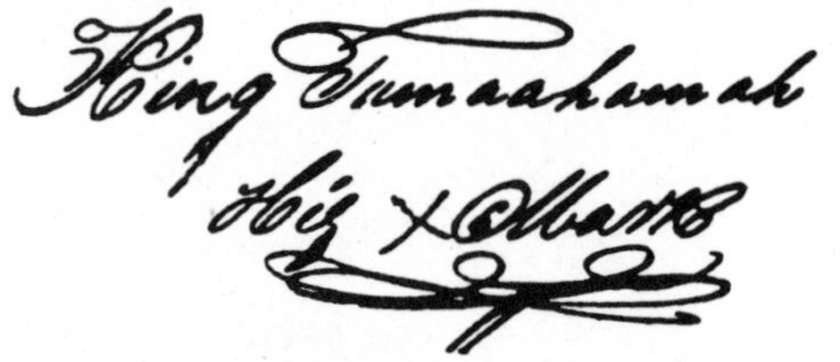

■ ■ ■ ■ ■ ■ ■ ■ ■ ■ ■ ■ ■ ■ ■ ■

King Tumaahamah
His X Marks

KING KAMEHAMEHA THE GREAT
1758-1819
Reigned: 1795-1819

Kamehameha

KING KAMEHAMEHA IV
(Alexander Lihiliho)
1834-1863
Reigned: 1854-1863

Rihoriho Iolani

KING KAMEHAMEHA II
(Rihoriho Iolani)
1797-1824
Reigned: 1819-1824

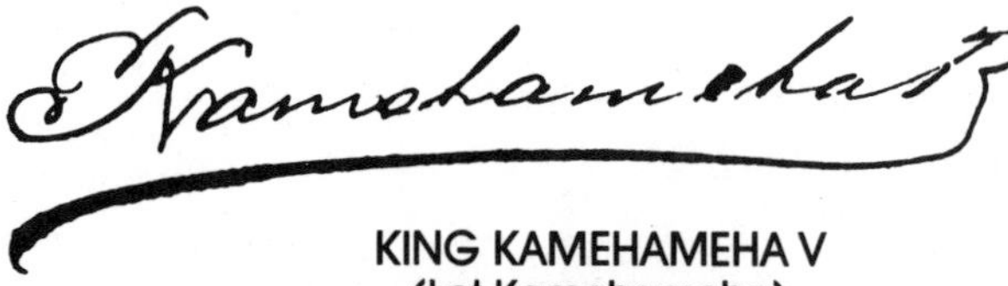

Kamehameha

KING KAMEHAMEHA V
(Lot Kamehameha)
1830-1872
Reigned: 1863-1872

Kamehameha

KING KAMEHAMEHA III
(Kauikeaouli)
1814-1854
Reigned: 1825-1854

KING LUNALILO
(William Charles Lunalilo)
1835-1874
Reigned: 1873-1874

KING KALAKAUA
(David Kalakaua)
1836-1891
Reigned: 1874-1891

QUEEN LILIUOKALANI
(Lydia Liliuokalani)
1838-1917
Reigned: 1891-1893

Paradise of the Pacific

ONE MODERN SIGNATURE

Leonard Mednick, MBA, CPA

Whata ya mean it's noon,
I just went to bed.

WHAT TIME IS IT THERE?

To determine the time in the countries listed, add or subtract the number of hours shown.

American Samoa	-1	Korea	+19
Andorra	+12	Liberia	+10
Argentina	+7	Liechtenstein	+11
Australia (Sydney)	+20	Luxembourg	+12
Bahrain	+13	Malaysia (Kuala Lumpur)	+18
Belgium	+12	Mexico	+4
Belize	+4	Monaco	+12
Bolivia	+6	Netherlands	+12
Brazil (Rio de Janeiro)	+7	Netherlands Antilles	+6
Chile	+6	New Zealand	+22
Colombia	+5	Nicaragua	+4
Costa Rica	+4	Norway	+11
Cyprus	+12	Papua, New Guinea	+20
Denmark	+11	Paraguay	+6
Ecuador	+5	Peru	+5
El Salvador	+4	Philippines	+18
Fiji Islands	+22	Portugal	+11
Finland	+12	Romania, Socialist Republic of	+12
France	+12	St. Barthelemy	+6
French Antilles	+6	San Marino	+12
German Democratic Republic	+11	Saudi Arabia	+13
Germany, Federation Republic of	+11	Singapore	+18
Greece	+13	South Africa, Republic of	+12
Guam	+20	Spain	+12
Guatemala	+4	Sweden	+11
Guyana	+7	Switzerland	+11
Haiti	+5	Taiwan	+18
Honduras	+4	Thailand	+17
Hong Kong	+18	Turkey	+13
Iceland	+10	United Kingdom	+11
Indonesia (Jakarta)	+17	U.S.S.R. (Moscow)	+13
Iran	+14	Uruguay	+7
Ireland	+11	Vatican City	+12
Israel	+12	Venezuela	+6
Italy	+12	Yugoslavia, Socialist Federal Republic of	+11
Japan	+19		
Kenya	+13		

Source: *Telephone directory; not adjusted for Daylight Savings.*

18 RULES FOR PROSTITUTES DURING WORLD WAR II

1. No visiting Waikiki at any time.
2. Cannot enter bars or better class cafes.
3. Cannot own property.
4. Cannot own an automobile.
5. Cannot have a steady boyfriend.
6. Cannot be seen on the streets with any man.
7. No dancing.
8. Cannot wire money to the mainland without the madam's permission.
9. No visiting a friend's apartment at any time.
10. No leaving the brothel after 10:30 p.m.
11. All army and navy posts kapu.
12. Cannot marry military personnel.
13. No outer island visits without permission.
14. Front seats of taxicabs kapu.
15. No shifting from one brothel to another.
16. Cannot visit golf courses.
17. No phoning the mainland without madam's permission.
18. Can swim only at Kailua Beach.

Source: *"My Life as a Honolulu Prostitute," by Betty Jean (Scarlet) O'Hara, based on rules set out by Police Chief William Gabrielson*

★★★★★★★

10 THINGS YOU DIDN'T KNOW ABOUT HAWAII AND WORLD WAR II

1. Fearing invasion, the U.S. government ordered all currency in circulation be replaced with bills overprinted with the word HAWAII, so that it could be declared illegal should it fall into enemy hands. All existing currency was destroyed—some $200 million, burned first in the crematory at Nuuanu cemetery, then in the sugar factory at Aiea.

2. In the days following the Pearl Harbor attack, divers recovered payrolls from the sunken ships. Because it was wet and oily, it was taken to a cleaning establishment where it was spun dry, but the bills curled up tightly to the diameter of a pencil. Pressing machines in commercial launderies were used to flatten the money.

3. Barbed wire was strung along Waikiki beach and the Royal Hawaiian Hotel was turned over to the military to be used by officers on R&R from the Pacific battle zone.

4. It took the government four days in December 1941 to strip the Lurline of her luxury and make a transport out of her capable of carrying more than 4,000 troops.

5. In 1944-45, there was an Italian prisoner-of-war camp near what is now Waikalua Road in Kaneohe.

Paradise of the Pacific

Paradise of the Pacific

6. On Dec. 6, 1941, Japanese warships were tuned in to Honolulu radio station KGMB, hoping to hear some warning if their proximity to the islands had been discovered.

7. The South Seas Economic Research Center, created by the Japanese Navy, envisioned Hawaii as a neutral country and proposed reinstating the Hawaiian monarchy under the protectorate of the Japanese government.

8. The late Bill Murata, an amateur magician, supported himself by performing for U.S. military units; because Japanese weren't allowed on base, he called himself Chew Gum Long (and got away with it!).

9. At some of the bars on Hotel Street, servicemen could have their pictures taken with a topless "hula" girl in a red-white-and-blue cellophane skirt, for $5.

10. There was an airfield where the Kualoa Ranch and Park are today, so you had to stop your car for takeoffs and landings.

■ ■ ■ ■ ■ ■ ■ ■ ■ ■ ■ ■ ■ ■

Paradise of the Pacific

□ □

20 STATES WITH "NO" VOTES ON STATEHOOD*

1. Alabama
(2 senators, 8 congressmen)
2. Arkansas (2 senators, 6 congressmen)
3. Florida (1 senator, 3 congressmen)
4. Georgia (2 senators, 8 congressmen)
5. Illinois (3 congressmen)
6. Kansas (1 congressman)
7. Kentucky (1 congressman)
8. Louisiana (1 senator, 1 congressman)
9. Michigan (4 congressmen)
10. Mississippi
(2 senators, 6 congressmen)

11. Missouri (1 congressman)
12. New York (5 congressmen)
13. Ohio (3 congressmen)
14. North Carolina (7 congressmen)
15. Pennsylvania (2 congressmen)
16. South Carolina
(2 senators, 3 congressmen)
17. Tennessee (2 congressmen)
18. Texas (16 congressmen)
19. Virginia (2 senators, 7 congressmen)
20. West Virginia (1 congressman)
*Total: 15 senators, 88 congressmen

Source: *Honolulu Star-Bulletin* reports,
March 12 & 13, 1959

Where Am I? Dept.
IF THIS IS HONOLULU, WHY AM I HAVING DINNER AT THE CALIFORNIA PIZZA KITCHEN?

1. The Paris Theater is in Chinatown
2. The University of Oklahoma has a branch at Hickam Air Force Base
3. The New York Technical Institute is in Kalihi
4. The New York Bakery is on Keeaumoku Street
5. The New Yorker Beauty Shop is in Kaimuki
6. Hong Kong Chop Suey is in Kealakekua, Hawaii
7. There are San Francisco Rag Shops at Ala Moana and Pearlridge
8. Tokyo Tailor is on Kapiolani Boulevard
9. So is the Hollywood Beauty College
10. The California Pizza Kitchen is in Kahala Mall
11. The New Tokyo Restaurant is in Waikiki
12. The Hong Kong Garage is Downtown

Sources: *Phone books & business directories*

10 OLDEST SCHOOLS

1. Lahainaluna . . . . 157 years
2. Royal School 149
3. Punahou School 147
4. St. Louis 142
5. Iolani School 125
6. Mid Pacific Institute 123
7. McKinley High School 122
8. St. Andrew's Priory 121
9. Haleiwa Elementary School 116
10. Ka'u (formerly Pahala
    Elementary School) 107

□ □ □

About 1,000 eye-teeth were needed to make an ankle rattle for use in the dance of the ancient hula—about as many would be found on 250 dogs. Today they use kupe'e shells.

U.S. Sen. Dan Inouye was working as a Civil Defense medical aide when shells fell on Pearl Harbor and he won a national prize for an article he wrote about his experience.

Nearly half of the land area of Hawaii is within five miles of the beach. The farthest point you can go inland from the sea is 28.5 miles, on the Big Island.

Paradise of the Pacific

20 ISLAND NAMES TO BROKE DA MOUT'

South Sea island names are followed, in parentheses, by the name of the island group.

1. Anuanuraro (Tuamoto)
2. Niuatoputapu Group (Tonga)
3. Tabiteuea (Gilbert)
4. Ailinglaplap (Marshall)
5. Agrihan (Northern Mariana)
6. Babeldaob (Palau)
7. D'Entre-Casteaux Reefs (New Caledonia)
8. Nukulaelae (Tuvalu)
9. Tabuaeran (Line)
10. Kwajalein (Marshall)
11. Mopihaa (Society)
12. Raivavae (Austral)
13. Nukunonu (Tokelau)
14. Nikumaroro (Kiribati)
15. Ngulu (Federated States of Micronesia)
16. Ngeaur (Palau)
17. Wotje (Marshall)
18. Kahoolawe (Hawaii)
19. Farallon de Medinilla (Northern Mariana)
20. Niuafo'ou (Tonga)

Source: *The New Pacific (map), published 1985 by Dept. of Planning & Economic Development; Geography & Map Div., Bernice P. Bishop Museum, and the Pacific Basin Development Council*

○○○○○○○○○○○○○○○○○○○○○○○○○○○○○○○

WHAT DID YOU DO IN THE PEACE, DADDY?
Former Peace Corps volunteers in Hawaii:

1. Randy Moore, president, Molokai Ranch; past president, Chamber of Commerce of Hawaii (Liberia)

2. Gregory Pai, chief economist, First Hawaiian Bank (Korea)

3. Ken Harding, Travel Industry Management dept. head, Hawaii Pacific College (Peru)

4. Barbara Fischlowitz, ran for state House in 1986 (Micronesia)

5. Trish Mahoney, Peace Corps recruiter, University of Hawaii (Thailand)

6. & 7. Joe and Chris Weldon, general manager, Sylvan Learning Centers (Peru)

8. Mike Schmicker, former editor, Hawaii Business magazine (Thailand)

9. & 10. Bryant and Susan Robey, public relations director, East West Center (Guinea)

11. Anson Chong, former state senator (Nigeria)

12. Jim Shon, state House (Korea)

13. Michael Gale, director, Hawaii District, Federal Action Agency (Venezuela)

Source: *Trish Mahoney (No. 5 above), whose list of Hawaii volunteers totals almost 250*

Next time you pass the Burger King on Kalakaua Avenue, corner of Lewers Street, look up at the second story of the building. In the 1940s and 1950s that space was occupied by the Beamer Hula Studio and it's where Shirley Temple learned to dance the hula for one of her early films.

Hawaii is moving closer to the Mainland at the rate of two inches a year.

THE HULA'S BUMMEST RAP!

"(It is) a very great and public evil, tending as we believe to demoralize the people very rapidly and very generally; to divert them from all industrial and intellectual pursuits; to lay waste their fields and gardens by neglect, as is actually the case in some places; to interfere materially with the prosperity of the schools; to foster idleness, dissipation, and licentiousness; to produce poverty and distress among the people, and thus create a strong temptation to supply their wants in unlawful ways; in short they (the hula) tend, we believe, to lead multitudes of the people back to that state of degradation in which this people once were..."

Source: *"Memorial" drafted by a number of missionaries for submission to Kamehameha V to get the hula banned, 1858*

All the residents of Pitcairn Island are descendants of the Bounty mutineers...and all are Seventh-day Adventists.

HOW THE BEACHES GOT THEIR NAMES

Oahu

1. SAN SOUCI: French for "without a care" and named for the resort built here in the 1880s—a favorite of Robert Louis Stevenson. Now called "Dig Me Beach" for the skimpy bathing suits.

2. SANDY BEACH: The only extensive sand beach on an otherwise rocky coast, it was called "the sand beach by the Blowhole," later Sand Beach and, finally, Sandy Beach or Sandy's.

3. POUNDERS BEACH: Named in the 1950s by the first students at the Church College of the Pacific (BYU) for the crushing shorebreak.

4. YOKAHAMA BEACH: Named by Japanese fishermen from the port city in Japan from which most Japanese immigrants to Hawaii had sailed.

5. QUEEN'S SURF: Once owned by Liliuokalani.

6. SUNSET BEACH: Named for a housing tract built in 1919 and stretching from Pupukea to what is now called Sunset Point; Sunset Tract was named for the sunsets viewed from the property.

Maui & Lanai

1. KAANAPALI BEACH: Takes the ancient name for the area, long out of use but revived by the developer, Amfac.

2. KAMAOLE I,II & III: Name means "childless," but origin of name is unknown.

3. SHIPWRECK BEACH: For the numerous wrecks, from the 1820s through the 1940s, when military landing craft ran aground on the reef.

Big Island

1. DISAPPEARING SANDS BEACH: Storms and high surf will take all the sand away in 24 hours.

2. GREEN SAND BEACH: Named for the tiny grains of olavine.

3. BLACK SAND BEACH: When hot lava hits cool ocean water, it explodes, becoming black sand.

Source: *Beaches of the Big Island, Beaches of Maui County and the Beaches of Oahu* by John R.K. Clark

60 HIGH SCHOOL TEAMS & WHAT THEY'RE CALLED

1. Academy of the Pacific .... Dolphins
2. Aiea High School .... Aliis
3. Baldwin High School .... Bears
4. Campbell High School .... Sabers
5. Castle High School .... Knights
6. Damien Memorial High School .... Monarchs
7. Farrington High School .... Governors
8. Hana High School .... Vikings
9. Hawaii Baptist Academy......................... Eagles
10. Hawaii Prepatory Academy .... Kamakanis
11. Hawaii School for Girls .... (None)
12. Hilo High School .... Vikings
13. Honokaa High School.......................... Dragons
14. Iolani School .... Red Raiders
15. Kahuku High School .... Red Raiders
16. Kailua High School............................. Surfriders
17. Kaimuki High School .... Bulldogs
18. Kaiser High School .... Cougars
19. Kalaheo High School .... Mustangs
20. Kalani High School............................... Falcons
21. Kamehameha School .... Warriors
22. Kapaa High School .... Warriors
23. Kau High School .... Trojans
24. Kauai High School .... Red Raiders
25. Kohala High School.............................. Cowboys
26. Konawaena High School .... Wildcats
27. Lahainaluna High School .... Lunas
28. Lanai High School............................... Pine Lads
29. Lanakila Baptist School .... Warriors
30. Laupahoehoe High School .... Seasiders

31. Leilehua High School .... Mules
32. Maryknoll High School .... Spartans
33. Maui High School .... Sabers
34. McKinley High School .... Tigers
35. Mid-Pacific Institute .... Owls
36. Mililani High School .... Trojans
37. Moanalua High School .... Menehunes
38. Molokai High School .... Farmers
39. Nanakuli High School .... Golden Hawks
40. Our Redeemer Lutheran School .... Lions
41. Pahoa High School .... Daggers
42. Parker School .... The Bulls
43. Pearl City High School....................... The Chargers
44. Punahou School .... Buff'n Blue
45. Radford High School .... Rams
46. Roosevelt High School .... Rough Riders
47. Sacred Hearts Academy .... Lancers
48. St. Andrew's Priory........................... Priory
49. St. Anthony High School .... Trojans
50. St. Francis High School .... (None)
51. St. Joseph High School .... Cardinals
52. St. Louis High School .... Crusaders
53. Seabury Hall.................................. (None)
54. Star of the Sea School .... Stars
55. University High School .... Jr. Rainbows
56. Waiakea High School .... Warriors
57. Waialua High School .... Bulldogs
58. Waianae High School .... Seariders
59. Waimea High School .... Menehunes
60. Waipahu High School .... Marauders

Source: *Hawaii High School Athletic Assn.*

41 OLYMPIANS LIVING IN HAWAII

Listed in alphabetical order, with year, sport and ranking

1. Thelma Kalama Aiu, Honolulu, 1948, swimming, GOLD
2. Adelaide Ballard, Honolulu, 1928, swimming, GOLD
3. John Beaumont, Honolulu, 1956, shooting, 9th
4. Brent Berk, Honolulu, 1968, swimming, 8th
5. Helen Cassidy, Honolulu, 1920, swimming
6. Richard Cleveland, Kihei, 1952, swimming
7. Richard Degener, Kihei, 1932 & 1936, swimming, BRONZE & GOLD
8. Peter George, Honolulu, 1948, 1952 & 1956 weightlifting, GOLD & 2 SILVER
9. Thomas Haine, Honolulu, 1968, volleyball
10. James Hardy, Hanalei, 1948, rowing, GOLD
11. Fanny Hopeau, Honolulu, 1968, volleyball
12. Emerick Ishikawa, Pearl City, 1948, weightlifting, 6th
13. Mariechen Jackson, Kamuela, 1924, swimming, GOLD & SILVER
14. Evelynn Konno, Honolulu, 1952, swimming, 2 BRONZE
15. Ford Konno, Honolulu, 1952 & 1956, swimming, 2 GOLD, 2 SILVER
16. Tommy Kono, Aiea, 1952 & 1960, weightlifting, 2 GOLD, 1 SILVER
17. Chokin Maekawa, Hili, 1956, boxing
18. Duncan Macdonald, Kailua, 1976, track
19. Micki McFadden, Honolulu, 1968, volleyball

Tommy Kono

Paradise of the Pacific

20. David McFaull, Honolulu, 1976, yachting, SILVER
21. Virginia Moore, Kamuela, 1968, kayak
22. George Onekea, Jr., Waipahu, 1956, swimming
23. Ray Perez, Honolulu, 1956, boxing
24. Barbara Perry, Honolulu, 1968, volleyball
25. Sharon Peterson, Hilo, 1968, volleyball

Duncan McDonald

Brett Uprichard

26. Pokey Richardson, Honolulu, 1964 & 1968, swimming, 2 GOLD

27. Mike Rothwell, Kailua, 1968, yachting, SILVER

28. William Smith, Kaneohe, 1948, swimming, 2 GOLD

29. Aileen Soule, Honolulu, 1920 & 1924, swimming, GOLD, BRONZE & SILVER

30. Allan Stack, Honolulu, 1948 & 1952, swimming, GOLD & 4th

31. Jon Stanley, Honolulu, 1968, volleyball

32. Richard Tanabe, Honolulu, 1956, swimming

33. Verneda Thomas, Honolulu, 1964 volleyball

34. Richard Tom, Honolulu, 1948 & 1952, weightlifting, BRONZE

35. Richard Tomita, Honolulu, 1948 & 1952, weightlifting, 9th

36. Carin Vanderbush, Wahiawa, 1956, swimming, SILVER

37. Pedro Velasco, Honolulu, 1964 & 1968, volleyball

38. Ken Walsh, Honolulu, 1968, swimming, 2 GOLD & 1 SILVER

39. Frank Walton, Honolulu, 1948, water polo

40. Keala Watson, Honolulu, 1968, swimming, BRONZE

41. William Woolsey, Kaneohe, 1952 & 1956, GOLD & SILVER & 6th

Source: *Peter George (see #8)*

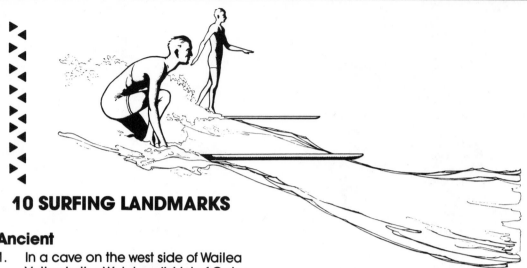

10 SURFING LANDMARKS

Ancient

1. In a cave on the west side of Wailea Valley in the Waialua district of Oahu lived a mo'o or serpent named Kalamainu'u, who gave her tongue to her husband to use as a surfboard. While surfing, he met a beautiful woman on a long board and was enticed to her cave, where they made love for several months, before the tired surfer, Puna'ai-koa'e, lost his good looks and returned to his mo'o wife.

2. Paiea challenged his Big Island chief, Umi, to a contest in the surf in front of Laupahoehoe, facing Hilo. When Paiea saw Umi winning, he crowded him against a rock, skinning the chief. Umi then pressed his foot against Paiea's chest and rushed ahead on the wave to win. The audience felt Paiea had been unfair and roasted him in an imu (oven) as punishment.

3. At Kooka, a wave spot located at Pua'a in North Kona on the Big Island, "where a coral head stands just outside a point of lava rocks," Kamehameha and his queen, Kaahumanu, rode the waves so that "only the light spray of the surf touched them before they reached the (shore)."

Modern:

1. A huge surf, generated by an earthquake in Japan in 1917, brought 30-foot waves to Waikiki, where Duke Kahanamoku and George "Dad" Center caught rides that took them for at least half a mile from takeoff point to the beach.

2. Waikiki was also where Jack London observed the "royal sport," in 1907: "Where but the moment before was only the wide desolation and invincible roar, is now a man, erect, full-statured, not-struggling frantically in that wild movement, not buried and crushed and buffeted by those mighty monsters, but standing above them all, calm and superb, poised on the giddy summit, his feet buried in the churning foam, the salt smoke rising to his knees, and all the rest of him in the free air and flashing sunlight, and he is flying through the air, flying forward, flying fast as the surge on which he stands. He is a Mercury—a brown Mercury. His heels are winged, and in them is the swiftness of the sea..."

3. In September, 1954, the First Makaha

Paradise of the Pacific

International Surfing Championships were held at Makaha Beach on Oahu's Leeward side, honoring Duke Kahanamoku. In 1970, surfer Fred Hemmings contributed and raised $6,000 for the first Smirnoff Pro-Am meet on this beach.

4. Waimea Bay on Oahu's North Shore, featured in many films, notably in "Ride the Wild Surf" (starring Tab Hunter as the surfer Steamer Lane), and mispronounced as Why-mee-ah Bay by the Beach Boys in their hit, "Surfin' U.S.A." Site of the "world's largest rideable waves."

5. Kammies, a surf break just west of Sunset Beach, named for the grocery store that provides the classic surfer's breakfast: a Twinkie and a Coke.

6. The Banzai Pipeline, at Ehukai Beach, site of Hawaii's most dangerous tubes; hundreds of surfers have been injured on the sharp coral and at least one has died, trapped in the underwater caves.

7. Kailua Beach, where Robbie Naish learned to windsurf, winning the first world championship while he was in the ninth grade, and won the next nine championships as well.

Source: *Ancient: 1 & 2, Sam Kamakau; 3, John Papa Ii. Modern: 1,3, & 4, Leonard Lueras, Surfing: The Ultimate Pleasure; 2, Jack London, "A Royal Sport: Surfing at Waikiki"; 5, 6, & 7, Author's files.*

SURF'S UP! TWENTY FEET
AND GLASSY!

Observations at Sunset Beach

Month	No. of days when flat or one foot	No. of days six feet or more
January	1	19
February	1	16
March	1	12
April	3	7
May	8	3
June	15	-
July	16	-
August	15	-
September	10	2
October	1	12
November	-	19
December	-	20
Totals:	71	110

Source: *Weather in Hawaiian Waters*
by Paul Haraguchi

12 CELEBRITY SURFERS

1. Lex Brodie
2. Malcom Ing (the ophthamologist)
3. William Simon (board chairman,
holding company that owns HonFed;
part-time resident)
4. Andy Bumatai (part-time resident)
5. Judge Michael Towne (Family Court)
6. Judge Eric Romanchek
(2nd Circuit, Maui)
7. Ricky Grigg (the oceanographer)
8. John DeSoto (City Councilman)
9. Warren Price (State Attorney General)
10. Joe Pynchon (Headmaster,
Hawaii School for Girls)
11. Tommy Holmes (author)
12. John Carroll

20 CELEBRITY GOLFERS

1. Gov. John Waihee
2. Former Gov. George Ariyoshi
3. Danny Kaleikini
4. Chief Justice Herman Lum
5. Mayor Frank Fasi
6. John Bellinger
7. Don Ho
8. R. Alex Anderson
9. Moe Keale
10. Police Chief Doug Gibb
11. Fire Chief Frank Kahoohanohano
12. Super lawyer Wally Fujiyama
13. Don Chapman
14. Councilwoman Donna Kim
15. Former Mayor Eileen Anderson
16. Andy Cummings
17. Ray Milici
18. Congressman Dan Akaka
19. Admiral Ronald Hays
20. Alan Beall

12 CELEBRITY RUNNERS
Marathoners marked with (M)

1. Council Chairman Arnold Morgado (M)
2. Lynne Waters
3. Joanne Yukimura
4. Katherine Luktenburg (M)
5. Dave Heenan, President, Theo H. Davies
6. Dick Jensen
7. Joyce Fasi
8. Jack Scaff (M)
9. Rep. Andy Levin (M)
10. Dr. Jack Lewin, Director, Dept of Health (M)
11. Hirohide Kamimura, CEO, JetTours Hawaii (M)
12. Kit Smith (M)

OTHER KINE
CELEBRITY JOCKS

1. Famous Amos, walking
2. Emme Tomimbang, horseback riding
3. Rep. Fred Hemmings,
   canoe paddling
4. Myron "Pinky" Thompson,
   canoe paddling
5. Bob Sevey, sailing
6. Judge Martin Pence, hunting
7. Tom Gentry, power boat racing
8. Tom Selleck, volleyball & softball
9. Don Chapman, softball
10. Bruce Stark, tennis
11. Nalani Blaisdell, canoe paddling
12. Bob Krauss, walking
13. Bernie Bays, rugby
14. Russ Francis, skydiving
15. John DeSoto, canoe paddling
16. John Finney, canoe paddling
17. Dr. Fred Fong, canoe paddling
18. Audy Kimura, skeet shooting
19. Fred Rolfing, swimming
20. Pat Bolen, triathlon

LOCAL OUT

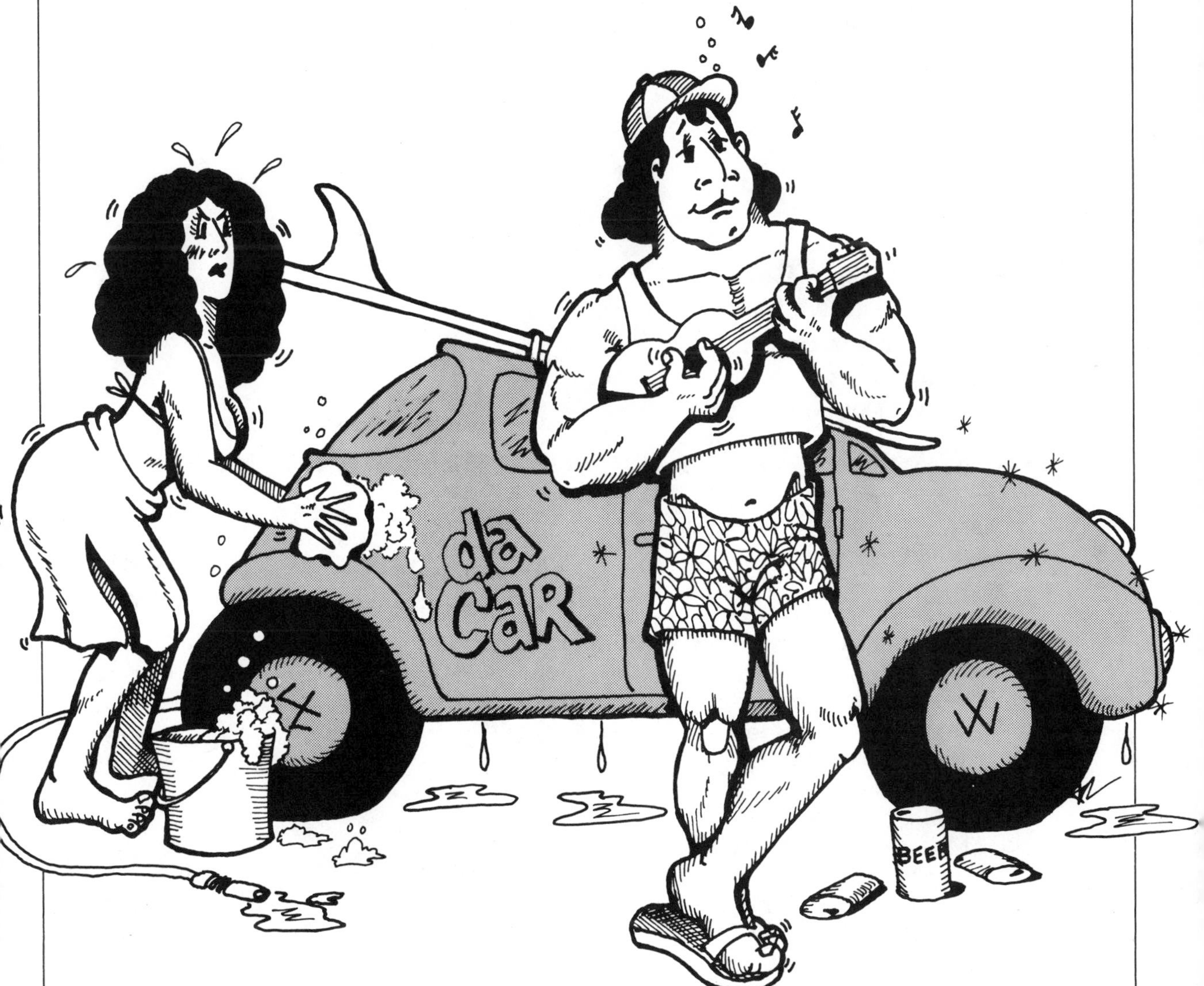

THAT'S FUNNY, YOU DON'T LOOK HAWAIIAN

How Hawaiian are they?

Andy Anderson, 1/4

Richard Smart, owner, Parker Ranch, 1/4

Kent Bowman, comic & president of TheoDavies Marine Agencies, 1/4

E.K. Fernandez, 1/4

John Henry Felix, president, Hawaiian Memorial Services, 1/32

Randy Lee, owner, Willows Restaurant, 1/4

Judge William Richardson, 3/8

Larry Mehau, president, Hawaii Protective Association, 1/2

Kenneth Brown, president, Mauna Lani Resort, 1/4

Fred Trotter, director, Campbell Estate, 1/16

Jack Magoon, CEO, Hawaiian Air Lines, 1/32

Aaron Chaney of Chaney, Brooks & Co., 3/16

John Bellinger, CEO, First Hawaiian, 1/4

John Waihee, 3/4

THERE IS ONLY 1 PURE HAWAIIAN AT KAM!

Pure	.04%
7/8	1.02%
3/4	2.69%
5/8	6.12%
1/2	11.66%
3/8	17.6%
1/4	29.69%
1/8	24.15%
1/16	7.07%

Source: *Kamehameha Schools, 1985-86, when there were 2,764 students*

INTER RACIAL MARRIAGE

Who the haole women married:

1. Haole men 52,434
2. Hawaiian men 4,134
3. Japanese men 2,505
4. Filipino men 2,235
5. Chinese men 1,105
6. Black men 452
7. Korean men 278
8. Samoan men 181
9. Other racial groups 1,229

Who the Japanese women married:

1. Japanese men 48,672
2. Haole men 5,101
3. Chinese men 1,996
4. Hawaiian men 1,677
5. Filipino men 1,254
6. Korean men 557
7. Black men 167
8. Samoan men 35
9. Other racial groups 487

Who the Hawaiian women married:

1. Hawaiian men 10,549
2. Haole men 4,554
3. Filipino men 1,921
4. Japanese men 1,258
5. Chinese men 699
6. Samoan men 212
7. Black men 199
8. Korean men 108
9. Other racial groups 493

Who the Filipino women married:

1. Filipino men 20,435
2. Haole men 3,067
3. Hawaiian men 1,095
4. Japanese men 844
5. Chinese men 241
6. Black men 180
7. Korean men 94
8. Samoan men 30
9. Other racial groups 342

Who the Korean women married:
1. Korean men 1,926
2. Haole men 1,150
3. Japanese men 580
4. Chinese men 193
5. Hawaiian men 141
6. Filipino men 134
7. Black men 36
8. Samoan men 0
9. Other racial groups 102

Who the Chinese women married:
1. Chinese men 8,015
2. Haole men 1,667
3. Japanese men 1,656
4. Hawaiian men 902
5. Filipino men 406
6. Korean men 185
7. Black men 43
8. Samoan men 19
9. Other racial groups 148

Who the Black women married:
1. Black men 2,116
2. Honkey men 126
3. Hawaiian men 16
4. Chinese men 13
5. Japanese men 12
6. Filipino men 7
7. Samoan men 0
8. Other racial groups 16

Who the Samoan women married:
1. Samoan men 1,405
2. Haole men 137
3. Hawaiian men 68
4. Filipino men 67
5. Japanese men 20
6. Chinese men 17
7. Black men 15
8. Korean men 0
9. Other racial groups 56

Source: *U.S. Census, 1980*

Camera Hawaii

△ △ △ △ △ △ △ △ △ △ △ △ △ △ △ △ △ △ △ △

8 MORMON FACTS

1. The Hawaiian LDS temple in Laie, built in 1919, was the first Mormon Temple to be built outside of the continental U.S. and was built in the form of a Greek cross, containing almost the exact cubical contents of the Temple of Solomon as mentioned in II Kings.

2. The steel guitar was invented by a Mormon, Joseph Kekuku, whose relatives still live in Laie.

3. The mosaic of the smiling Christ at the Honolulu LDS Tabernacle building on Beretania St. (at the corner of Punahou St.) was the largest representation of Christ in the world at that time (1941) and is still one of the largest in the world.

4. In a recent survey, only 28 percent of Mormons questioned said they always or usually read scriptures daily, and 29 percent said they always had daily prayer; many parents said they wanted to be more consistent in these areas, but with an average of six children, they found it very difficult to get all family members together at the same time.

5. In the same survey, 79 percent of the fathers said they had not gone on a mission.

6. Henry Bigler, a Mormon missionary, was one of the first people to discover gold at the Mormon colony at Sutters Fort, Sacramento, Calif., in 1849.

7. "The Hukilau Song" ("I'm going . . . to a hukilau . . . to a huki-huki-huki-huki-huki-lau . . .") was written by a Canadian tourist, Jack Owens, after a visit to the Morman Laie hukilau in 1949.

8. One of the first missionaries to Hawaii from the Mormon church was George Cannon, who arrived on a Monday in Keanae on Maui, and by Wednesday had baptized more than 130 persons.

Sources: *(1, 2, 3, 6, & 7) Ishmael Stagner; (4 & 5) Effective Mormon Families by William G. Dyer & Phillip R. Kunz; Hawaii: an Uncommon History by Edward Joesting.*

WHO'S GOT THE GOOD JOBS?
(BY ETHNIC GROUP)

Job Category	Total Jobs	Haw'n.	Jap.	Chin.	Cauc.	Filip.
Management	12,370	7.2%	40.5%	10.4%	30.7%	6.9%
Teachers	13,650	6.7%	45.2%	8.6%	31.3%	1.0%
Clerical	18,630	8.5%	41.2%	6.7%	31.3%	1.0%
Police, Firemen	3,158	29.9%	17.9%	6.8%	31.2%	6.4%
Farm, Forest, Fishing	14,154	13.7%	22.6%	1.9%	22.7%	33.3%
Construct	20,977	11.8%	36.0%	3.2%	29.1%	14.2%
Food Svcs.	32,461	11.0%	24.7%	9.0%	27.3%	17.6%

Source: *Hawaii Business, April 1985, based on U.S. Census, 1980*

CANCER RATES, BY ETHNIC GROUP

Comparing Haoles, Chinese, Filipinos, Hawaiians & Japanese

1. Filipinos have the lowest cancer rates among the five groups.
2. Hawaiians have the highest overall rates. Smoking causes twice the rate of cancer among Hawaiians that it does among Filipinos.
3. Japanese have the highest rates of stomach, colon and rectal cancer. Stomach cancer rates are lower for Americans of Japanese ancestry in Hawaii than for Japanese nationals, but AJAs have a higher incidence of breast and colon cancer.
4. Haoles in Hawaii have the highest rate of skin cancer among all groups, but fare better for all cancers than caucasians on the Mainland.
5. Chinese have the highest rate of nose and throat cancer.
6. Chinese-Filipinos have the best survival rate for lung cancer.

Source: *Pacific Foundation for Cancer Research, 1986*

HOW MANY TEENAGERS, BY ETHNIC GROUP

Hawaiian/
Part Hawaiian ..... 34,166 .... 30%
Japanese .... 20,430 .... 18%
Caucasian .... 18,407 .... 16%
Filipino .... 14,918 .... 13%
Chinese .... 3,518 .... 3%
Other .... 21,686 .... 20%

Total 113,125

*Source: Office of Children & Youth,
Office of the Governor*

TEENAGE MOMS, BY ETHNIC GROUP (AGE 12-18)

Hawaiian 32
Part-Hawaiian 770
Japanese 231
Caucasian 509
Filipino 338
Chinese 46
Korean 29
Black 30
Samoan 46
Portuguese 26
Spanish/Puerto Rican 43
Indochinese 23
Other Pacific Islanders 8
Unknown 55

Total 2,240

Source: Hawaii State Dept. of Health

HABLA EL TAGALOG
(Who speaks what, on Oahu)

Total population
 (age 5 and over) 887,707
Speak only English at home 658,752
Speak a language other than
 English at home 228,955
What language?
Japanese 80,230
Filipino languages 66,655
Chinese 20,066
Spanish 11,933
Samoan 11,020
Korean 9,231
Hawaiian 9,060
Tongan 1,180
Other Polynesian 480
Other 19,100

Source: *U.S. Census*

Paradise of the Pacific

THE HIGH COST OF DYING

Mortuary	Standard burial	Standard casket	Direct cremation
Oahu			
Associate Memorial Group:	$1,804	$818	$544
Diamond Head Mortuary			
Kukui Mortuary			
Nuuanu Memorial Park Mortuary			
Windward Mortuary			
Care Group:	1,610	511	523
Hawn. Memorial Park Mortuary			
Williams Mortuary			
Hosoi Garden Mortuary	1,487	1,295	478
Borthwick Mortuary	1,347	780	541
Leeward Funeral Home	1,144	780	416
Big Island			
Memorial Mortuary	1,072	574	415
Hawaii Funeral Home	1,066	1,196	442
Dodo Mortuary	998	1,139	499
Maui			
Maui Mortuary Bulgo's/Norman's	1,347	780	541
Nakamura's Mortuary	1,078	830	468
Kauai			
Kauai Mortuary	1,319	593	447
Garden Island Mortuary	1,009	962	489
Molokai			
Molokai Mortuary	827	744	300

1. *Standard burial:* excludes casket, but includes funeral counseling, pickup of deceased, refrigeration and/or embalming, transportation, use of mortuary for two days, and if available, beverage service, organist, guest book, acknowledgement cards, and pallbearers' gloves.
2. *Standard casket:* is the largest-selling casket in Hawaii, Model 300, white Chatham, made by Honolulu Casket Co.
3. *Direct cremation:* is cremation without formal viewing, visitation or ceremony, including pickup of deceased, transportation to crematory, death certificate, counseling to family, and cremation.

Source: *Honolulu mortuaries*

WHERE DA "BRAINS" ARE— BY NEIGHBORHOOD

• • • • • •

Neighborhood	High School	College
1. Palolo	36.3%	7.5%
2. Wahiawa	43%	9%
3. Nanakuli	27.4%	3.6%
4. McCully/ Moiliili	38.1%	17.4%
5. Ala Moana	41.2%	13.8%
6. Kapalama	33.3%	4.8%
7. Waipahu	37.6%	7.4%
8. Waialua/ Haleiwa	37.2%	8.0%
9. Waianae Valley	32.0%	6.0%
10. Kahuku	25.0%	10.9%
11. Whitmore Village	23.3%	3.9%
12. Date/Citron	44.2%	14.8%
13. Maili	33.2%	4.1%
14. Kinau/ Vineyard	33.2%	14.5%
15. Pensacola/ Makiki	40.2%	21.7%
16. Waimanalo	37.1%	6.0%
17. Kalihi	33.3%	6.2%
18. Palama	31.9%	8.0%
19. Lower Kalihi	26.5%	4.8%

Source: *Office of Human Resources*

20 MOST DANGEROUS SCHOOLS
Juvenile Arrests (1986)

Heavy-duty crime (murder, man-slaughter, rape, robbery, aggravated assault, burglary, larceny-theft, auto theft)

1. Kalakaua Intermediate School 233
2. Farrington High School 178
3. McKinley High School 161
4. Kaimuki High School 153
5. Waianae High School 132
6. Dole Intermediate School 107
7. Waipahu High School........... 105
8. Aiea High School 96
9. Castle High School 82
10. Radford High School 77

Not-so-heavy-duty crime (other assaults, arson, forgery & counterfeiting, fraud, embezzlement, stolen property, vandalism,weapons, prostitution, sex offenses, drug laws, gambling, offenses against family, DUI, disorderly conduct)

1. McKinley High School 350
2. Farrington High School 325
3. Waianae High School 285
4. Kaimuki High School 256
5. Campbell High School 213
6. Castle High School 203
   Waipahu High School 203
7. Roosevelt High School........... 202
8. Pearl City High School 194
9. Kalakaua Intermediate School.......................... 191
10. Mililani High School 184

Source: *Honolulu Police Dept., Annual Statistical Report, 1986*

Paradise of the Pacific/Floye Garrison

MOST ARRESTS, BY ETHNIC GROUP

		Under 18	Over 18	Total
1.	Haole	1,896	10,138	12,034
2.	Hawaiian	3,610	4,940	8,550
3.	Filipino	1,490	2,960	4,450
4.	Japanese	596	2,061	2,657
5.	Samoan	817	1,532	2,349
6.	Black	215	1,674	1,889
7.	Chinese	117	616	713
8.	Korean	128	416	544
9.	Other	1,697	2,993	4,690

Source: *Honolulu Police Department, Annual Statistical Report, 1986*

16 MISCELLANEOUS FACTS

1. Does your dad have the letters KHB tattooed on his arm? It could stand for Koolau Boys' Home, the youth correctional center in Kailua—that was a popular tattoo for the KBH inhabitants in the 1950s.

2. Doris Duke's mansion at Black Point has lanai doors that drop into slots in the ground.

3. Many of the macadamia nuts sold in Hawaii are grown in Kenya, Costa Rica and Brazil.

4. One out of every 10 people in Hawaii is illiterate.

5. What's the skin that peels off after a bad sunburn called? Blype.

6. Hawaii is the only state with no incorporated towns.

7. The best-selling Hawaiian record album is Honolulu City Lights by the Beamer Brothers, Keola and Kapono, released in 1979 on Bluewater Records (owned by promoter Tom Moffatt) and still selling briskly in LP, cassette and CD. Total sold so far (according to Keola) is more than 250,000 copies. Most Hawaiian records sell fewer than 5,000 copies today.

8. Ronald Reagan is allergic to flowers, so when he was here (for his honeymoon and later, just before he declared for president), he was given kukui nut leis.

Paradise of the Pacific

9. John Bellinger, Robert Pfeiffer and David Murdock, the top guns at the Bank of Hawaii, Alexander & Baldwin, and Castle & Cook, respectively, don't have a college degree between them.

10. The orchid is named after the male genitalia. Its botanical family name, Orchidacaea, means "testicles" in Greek. (Which may derive from an early notion that the orchid was an aphrodisiac.)

11. When Jack Lord was a student at the famed Actor's Studio in New York, his fellow students included Marilyn Monroe, Maureen Stapleton, Paul Newman and Marlon Brando.

12. The City of Honolulu collects between $8,000 and $20,000 a day from its parking meters, depends on the season. Christmas no ka oi.

13. A whale's heart beats only nine times a minute.

14. If you have trouble with spelling, be advised that Captain Cook wrote Hawaii as Owy-hee, Maui as Mowee, Oahu as O-ahoo, Kauai as Atowai, and Niihau as Neehau.

15. All new street neames in Hawaii must be given Hawaiian names. 86 percent already have them.

16. The bufo population is shrinking fast. Some people blame the cattle egret. They'll eat anything.

HOW MANY ARE THERE?

1. Six-packs of beer hauled away by trash collectors every Christmas .120,000
2. Monkeys in the Pearl City Tavern Monkey Bar 14
3. Kinds of fish in Hawaiian waters 650
4. Hostess bars 400
5. Stolen cars (annually) 3,258
6. Local telephone calls (daily) 2,200,000
7. Hospital beds 6,595
8. Handguns (registered) 3,687
9. Tourists in Waikiki on an average day 75,000
10. Farms 4,595
11. Abortions (annually) 5,647
12. Bankruptcies (annually) 782
13. Dogs (licensed) 18,713
14. Millionaires 800
15. Honeymoons (annually) 316,000
16. Rapes (annually) 240
17. Food stamp households 35,652
18. Gallons of water used by family of four every two month billing period 24,000
19. Deaths by drowning (annually) . . 25
20. Senators and Congressmen who voted against statehood (see HISTORY & GEOGRAPHY) 104

Source: *(1) Honolulu Dept. of Public Works; (2) Pearl City Tavern; (3) Know Hawaii; (4) Liquor Commission; (5) Honolulu Police Dept.; (6) Hawaiian Telephone Co.; (7) State Dept. of Health; (8) Honolulu Police Dept.; (9) Hawaii Visitors Bureau; (10) U.S. Census; (11) State Dept. of Health; (12) Admin. Officer of the U.S. Courts; (13) Honolulu Dept. of Finance; (14) Internal Revenue Service; (15) Modern Bride Magazine; (16) Honolulu Police Dept.; (17) Dept. of Social Services & Housing; (18) Board of Water Supply; (19) State Dept. of Health; (20) U.S. Congress*

Brett Uprichard

■ ■ ■ ■ ■ ■ ■ ■ ■ ■ ■

The military families in Hawaii account for about 10 percent of the population and 21 percent of the birthrate. On the other hand, Don Ho has 8 kids and Frank Fasi has 11.

In 1980, we had 50,000 native Californians living in Hawaii and more than 115,000 native Hawaiians living in California.

Bishop Estate Trustee William Richardson, who is ⅜ Hawaiian, didn't go to Kamehameha School because his parents didn't think the curriculum was strong enough to get him into college.

■ ■ ■ ■ ■ ■ ■ ■ ■ ■ ■

There are three brothers in Lahaina whose last name is Silva. Their first names are Sterling, Quick and Hiyo.

9 WAYS TO SAY "I LOVE YOU"

1. Samoan: *Oute alofa iate oe*
2. Korean: *Sarang hamnida*
3. Ilocano: *Ay-ayatenka*
4. Tagalog: *Iniibig kita*
5. Japanese: *Aishite imasu*
6. Cantonese: *Or oy ne*
7. Hawaiian: *Aloha*
8. Thai: *Sawadee krap*
9. Pidgin: *You like make babies?*